Happy Healthy
DOGs

Slim Dogs Live Longer

Curtis Willauer D.V.M., Barbara Ota, M.S.
and Cameron Stauth
with Steven Rosenblatt PhD., M.D.

Finally! A Practical Way for
Dogs to Lose Weight!

Introducing the
Future of Canine Weight Control:

The Starch Blocker Strategy

Copies of this book may be purchased for educational, business, or sales promotional use. For information, please write: SierraMed Publishing Co., 2029 Century Park East, Suite 1112, Los Angeles, California 90067

FOR MORE INFORMATION CONTACT:
Steven Rosenblatt Ph.D., M.D., President,

Vet Medicinals, Inc.
2029 Century Park East, Suite 1112
Los Angeles, CA 90067.
www.sierramed.com
www.vetmedicinals.com

ISBN 0-9760580-0-6

FIRST EDITION   1

TABLE OF CONTENTS

Introduction
by Steven Rosenblatt, M.D., Ph.D.

It is my carefully considered clinical opinion that the recent scientific breakthrough known as starch blockers represents the best new approach for weight management for not only people, but also for dogs. It is important to note that some of the earliest studies on the effectiveness of starch blockers for weight loss were done on dogs.

It is not particularly unusual for health products that were created for human use to be applied to animals. For example, antibiotics were created for human use, but are generally equally effective among most animals, including dogs. Similarly, many of the vitamin and mineral supplements that are appropriate for humans are also appropriate for dogs.

This principle of dual effectiveness applies to starch blockers. Humans and dogs both consume relatively high levels of starch, and both metabolize it in much the same way. In both humans and dogs, starch accounts for approximately 25% to 33% of the average daily diet, and is digested primarily by a pancreatic enzyme called alpha amylase.

Starch blockers, known commercially as Phase 2™, temporarily inhibit the digestion of this dietary starch. When a person or a dog consumes a small amount of Phase 2™ – which is a natural, organic partial-protein derived from white beans – the Phase 2™ joins with the starch-digesting enzyme amylase for approximately one hour. In effect, the Phase 2™ puts amylase in a chemical "headlock," preventing it from breaking down starch molecules.

Therefore, most of the starch that is eaten at this time passes through the system in a whole-molecule form, without releasing its calories, in almost exactly the same way that fiber does. Fortunately, all the other nutrients in the starchy food, including its vitamins and minerals, are digested normally. There are no significant side-effects.

There has never before been a weight management approach that has been so elegantly simple, but so profoundly powerful. Almost all other approaches rely upon stimulating the metabolism, or altering brain chemistry. Not Phase 2™. It has only one, limited action – inhibition of starch calorie digestion – but it performs this single action with stunning efficiency.

I was first introduced to the Phase 2™ method of weight management in 2002, when I read several studies about it in scientific journals. I soon began recommending this non-prescription supplement to my patients, and many of them achieved remarkable results. Patients who had been unable to lose weight on restrictive, self-denial diets were suddenly able to shed unwanted pounds. They did not have to drastically alter their lifestyles or eating patterns. They just had to introduce this new supplement into their daily routines. For the first time in the lives of many of these people, they did not have to suffer to be thin. They could eat normal foods in normal amounts and still lose weight, simply because most of their starch calories were being blocked by Phase 2™.

Of course, these people still needed to be sensible about eating too much fat or sugar, because Phase 2™ has no effect upon these foodstuffs. It blocks only the calories in starch. However, because most of my patients were consuming about one-fourth to one-third of their daily calories as starch, inhibiting these calories effectively triggered weight loss.

For most of these patients, Phase 2™ inhibited the absorption of about 500-750 calories per day, and this was enough to cause weight loss in most people. Losing one pound of fat requires the avoidance (or the burning) of approximately 3000 calories, so blocking 500 calories each day generally results in about one pound of body-fat loss every six days.

As my patient population flourished with this new approach, I began to think that starch blockers might have an even broader application. I wondered, "Why can't this same approach be applied to companion animals?" I was aware that there was an obesity epidemic among pets, because my good friend Barbara Ota, O.M.D., M.S. – the co-author of this book – had brought it to my attention. She had pointed out that the obesity epidemic in companion animals had closely paralleled the unfolding obesity epidemic among humans.

Her theory, which has been endorsed by many other animal clinicians, was that America's pets had become too fat over the past 20 years mostly because of the introduction of high-starch pet foods, made primarily from grains. Dogs had evolved as carnivores over hundreds of thousands of years, she said, and the recent trend of feeding them mostly high-grain dog foods was contradictory to their evolutionary biology.

This theory seemed to be compatible with the concept that the human obesity epidemic of the past 20 years has also been triggered mostly by the over consumption of carbohydrates.

I knew that Phase 2™ starch blockers were notably effective for people, and I was almost certain they would be equally effective for dogs. The reason I was so confident that starch blockers would work for dogs was because much of the early research on them had involved dogs, which had been used as surrogates for humans. The Mayo Clinic, in particular, had done several very successful studies involving dogs. The research there had shown conclusively that starch blockers had the same effect upon dogs as humans.

Based upon these many years of preliminary research, I helped Dr. Ota and her colleague Curtis Willauer, D.V.M., design a study of canine weight management, using starch blockers. The results of that study were spectacular, as you will see in this book.

Since that initial study, others have been commissioned, and additional evidence has indicated unequivocally that Phase 2™ can effectively promote weight loss among dogs.

The importance of this breakthrough in canine obesity can not be overstated. Similarly to humans, the canine body simply can not tolerate obesity. Obese dogs tend to suffer from the same constellation of diseases that plague obese humans: cardiovascular disease, diabetes, cancer, joint disorders, liver dysfunction, fatigue, heat intolerance, and pancreatic problems. Obesity significantly shortens the lives of dogs, just as it does humans.

Phase 2™ starch blockers, currently marketed under the brand name VetSlim, offer a scientifically sound method of preventing the diseases associated with canine obesity.

This approach is not a substitute for a sensible diet and exercise program. It is simply an important part of that program. As such, it is the best possible approach to a new and frightening problem: the premature deaths and unnecessary suffering, due to obesity, of America's beloved pet population.

References:

1) Tamadera, K, et.al., Mayo Clinic, "Can chronic ingestion of a wheat amylase inhibitor reduce insulin secretion without producing malabsorption in dogs?" Pancreas, Vol. 7 No. 6 p. 762, 1992.

2) Koike, D., et. al., Mayo Clinic, "Effect of a wheat amylase inhibitor on canine carbohydrate digestion, gastrointestinal function, and pancreatic growth," Gastroenterology, Vol. 108, No. 4, 1995.

Chapter One

Welcome To The New World Of Canine Weight Control

You'll Learn:

- Why so many dogs are overweight.
- Why it's so dangerous for them.
- Why excessive grain in their food is making them fat.

- **How you can solve all these problems with starch blockers!**

Toby was miserable! Poor dog!

Toby was a dachshund, shaped along the lines of a super sized Tootsie Roll, who was carrying far more weight than his lengthy back could handle. Every time Toby tried to move, he would whine and cringe. Some of the disks in his vertebrae were pushed out of their proper positions, due to the extra baggage that puffed up Toby's sides and belly, and this caused him to have severe, chronic back pain. Joint pain is extremely common among overweight dogs.

At Toby's veterinary clinic, the Director of Complementary Medicine, Barbara Ota, was quite concerned. This would not be an easy case. And Toby's guardian, Pam, was far more than concerned. She was terrified. Pam knew that she couldn't allow Toby to suffer this degree of pain indefinitely. If Pam couldn't find a way to help relieve the source of Toby's chronic pain, she knew she would soon have to let go of the dog she loved so much, and lose Toby forever. "Toby's still so cute," Pam murmured, running her hands over Toby with obvious affection. "And he isn't even very old yet."

Barbara Ota didn't agree that Toby looked cute – but this wasn't the time to say so. Toby didn't look cuddly to Barbara – he looked fat. Because Toby was fat.

Toby's guardian saw her dog through the eyes of love – and perceived every excess ounce of him as just that much more to adore. To her, the rolls of fat that ringed Toby's midsection were just reminders of the many tasty treats she'd showered upon her dog.

But Barbara saw Toby from the perspective of a scientist, and saw the rings of excess fat as deadly threats to the dog's well-being and life. Barbara suspected that Pam was literally killing Toby with kindness – shortening the life of the dog she loved by trying to express her love with food. The result was a dog layered with excess fat.

Barbara was seeing this condition occur with alarming regularity – and with terrible consequences. Barbara was painfully aware of the following facts:

- 25% of all dogs in America are obese. Not just cuddly or plump. Obese. Also, approximately 40% are overweight, and many of them are quickly becoming obese.

- This canine obesity is dangerous and deadly. Many veterinarians consider obesity to be the number one physical problem among dogs.

- The obesity epidemic in dogs is relatively new. It was not a frightening, nationwide crisis 25 years ago.

- A huge contributing factor to the obesity epidemic in dogs is excessive carbohydrate intake -- just as excessive carb consumption now plays a major role in the human obesity epidemic.

Above all else, Barbara knew this:

Dogs are primarily carnivorous.
They do not require carbohydrates.
But most modern dog foods are packed with carbs,
in the form of grains.

"Toby needs to lose weight," Barbara told Pam. Based upon tests and observations, Barbara believed that Toby was approximately 25% above her ideal body weight. This placed Toby clearly in the category of being not just overweight, but obese – and not far from being morbidly obese.

Pam swallowed, and looked ill at ease. "I know he's a little chubby," Pam said. "And I've tried to help her slim down. But it's hard. It's harder for me to keep his weight down than it is for me to keep my own weight down, because I know how important weight is, and Toby doesn't have any way of knowing. All Toby knows is that he loves to eat, and whenever I don't give him as much food as he wants, he just looks at me with those big eyes, like, "Don't you love me anymore?"

Barbara nodded sympathetically. She lived in the real world. She knew the bond that food created between pets and their guardians, and she knew that dogs were often skillful at manipulating their so-called "masters" into giving them excessive amounts of food – to the point where it begged the question: Who was " mastering" whom? In the past, Barbara might have despaired. She had lost so many wonderful animals to the complications of obesity. But on this day, she had a new secret weapon. Every indication was that this new weapon against obesity was remarkably effective for dogs. It might also work for cats – though research specifically on cats hadn't yet been performed.

The new weapon was the substance, already approved for human use, known as starch blockers.

Starch blockers are the extraordinary new weight control solution used by millions of people. Now they are also being used for canine weight control.

The Starch Blocker Strategy

Starch blockers are an exciting new approach to weight control that have thus far been used mostly by humans. Veterinary studies and clinical veterinary practice show, however, that starch blockers are equally effective for triggering canine weight loss.

Starch blockers are a natural partial protein, derived from organic white beans. When ingested in a pill, powder, chew, or capsule form, they bind with the starch-digesting enzyme in human, and canine, bodies for approximately one hour. Any starch eaten during that hour passes through the system in a whole-molecule form, exactly as fiber does, without releasing any calories. All of the other nutrients in the starchy foods – including vitamins, minerals, protein, and essential fatty acids – are metabolized normally. The only effect of starch blockers is to neutralize approximately two-thirds to three-fourths of all starch calories. Starch blockers have been proven to have absolutely no side-effects, and no toxicity whatsoever. They do not cause stimulation, habituation, or disruption of normal metabolic processes.

Starch blockers have been tested for more than 30 years at a wide range of universities and hospitals throughout America and abroad, including the Mayo Clinic, the University of Illinois, and at hospitals associated with U.C.L.A. They were introduced commercially for human use in 2003 and were an instant sensation. Following publication of The Starch Blocker Diet – by Steven Rosenblatt, M.D., Ph.D., and Cameron Stauth – they became America's most popular diet strategy, far outpacing all other diets, including even Atkins and South Beach, which have thus far surpassed starch blockers in media attention, but not in number of adherents or in product sales. There are currently more than 250 different brand-name starch blocker products, with an annual worldwide sales of approximately $300 million. They are now sold on every continent. Sales continue to grow geometrically, having increased by 900% during the latter part of 2003.

In the "Age of Atkins" – the current era of widespread avoidance of carbohydrates -- starch blockers provide the only existing alternative to conventional food-denial dieting, for humans as well as dogs. They allow people and dogs to eat starchy foods without absorbing the heavy load of calories these foods carry. The average person eats about 25% of his or her diet as starch, so use of starch blockers exerts an already powerful reduction on caloric intake, without disrupting or denying normal dietary habits or desires. Similarly, dogs currently eat large amounts of starchy foods. Starch calories generally comprise about 40% of the average dog's diet. Most of these starch calories come from grain-based dry dog foods, some come from canned food, and some come from table scraps.

Besides adding hundreds of calories to daily diets – for dogs as well as humans – starch has recently been shown in numerous studies to be disruptive to the metabolism. It is transformed by the bodies of both people and dogs into pure sugar within minutes of being eaten. Many forms of starch, including many of the starches found in common dog foods, enter the bloodstream even faster than table sugar does. The primary rationale for virtually all low-carb diets -- including Atkins, The South Beach Diet, The Zone, Protein Power, and Sugar Busters – is that this metabolic disruption of blood sugar (and insulin) triggers a multitude of metabolic problems, including hunger and poor insulin function.

This same harmful effect on metabolism has been proven to occur in dogs. In fact, most of the early research on starch blockers, including thirteen separate studies performed at Mayo Clinic, used dogs as the research model, and appeared to suggest that dogs do not thrive in a grain-based diet. In addition, very recent research, conducted by this book's authors, confirmed the findings of Mayo Clinic that showed starch blockers effectively enable dogs to lose weight, with no side-effects.

Equally as important is the observation that the dogs who lost weight taking starch blockers did so with no apparent hunger or dissatisfaction. In conventional canine weight loss regimens, it is very common for dogs to show signs of hunger, such as begging for food, whining, acting lethargic, or demanding undue attention. These behaviors did not occur to a significant degree in dogs taking starch blockers. This quality of life issue, of course, is of great importance to the guardians of dogs -- as well as to the dogs themselves.

Thus, using starch blockers for canine weight management opens a vast new vista in veterinary practice, and in dog guardianship. For the first time, pet guardians can give their dogs the foods the dogs want, on a long-term basis, without paying the terrible price of eventually losing to illness the animals they were only trying to love.

There's nothing magical about the way starch blockers work. They are characterized merely by good science, and good sense. But they can have an almost magical effect upon dogs, and upon those dogs' relationships with the people who love them.

It was eight weeks after Toby's first visit to Barbara. Toby had lost more than three pounds -- a tremendous achievement in an animal that had weighed only 13 pounds to begin with.

Toby had been given a small amount of powdered starch blocker with each meal, and it had made a tremendous difference in the dog's weight and health. Best of all, Toby hadn't even appeared to notice that she was metabolizing fewer calories each day. He'd shown no signs of hunger, and had even seemed to be more satisfied and content with her feedings than he'd been before the starch blocker regimen. Gone were the rings of fat that had bunched up Toby's skin and fur. Barbara could clearly see the healthy outlines of Toby's ribs.

Toby scampered about playfully, devoid of any signs of chronic back pain caused by obesity. Pam said that Toby had been "acting like a puppy again." Pam exultantly lifted her beloved dog and patted Toby's newly taut belly. "Look at this!" Pam said, pointing at the dog's tight, exposed midsection. "Toby's got a six-pack!"

Barbara laughed. On this day, she had a lot to feel good about.

Chapter Two

How Obesity Happens

You'll Learn:

- How healthy dogs gradually gain weight.
- How excessive grain content in some dog foods can trigger weight gain.
- Why so many dogs now get diabetes.

- **What you can do to solve these problems – without depriving your dog!**

Dogs, in so many ways, are similar to people – probably more similar than you realized.

In fact, recent findings at the Institute for Genomic Research indicate that humans have more genes in common with dogs than they do with the animal that is most often used for human health studies: the mouse. The Genome Map shows that dogs have 18,473 genes that correspond exactly to the 24,567 human genes. In other words, humans are approximately 75% genetically identical to dogs.

This means, said the director of the study, Dr. Lawrence Schook, that "Information about human diseases can be used to treat dogs, and understanding dog diseases can be used to help humans." Dr. Schook also noted that, "Dogs, like humans, get diseases associated with lifestyles. Thus, not exercising and overeating can result in obesity and diabetes in both dogs and humans." The physical link between canine and human physiology has never been more clear than it is in the ongoing studies of overweight and obesity. In this field, dogs are commonly used as the animal model for research that is intended to benefit humans. As we previously mentioned, most of the studies done on starch blockers at Mayo Clinic were performed with dogs as the research animal. These studies, and others like them, revealed a fascinating connection between the ways that humans become over-weight and the ways that dogs become overweight. It has now become apparent, as the study of carbohydrates has intensified, that excessive carbs can be every bit as harmful to dogs as over consumption of carbs is to humans.

Ironically, these studies on man's best friend have now put people in the position to become their dogs' best friends, by enabling them to know *how to feed their dogs right*.

**Dogs get fat the same way people do: gradually --
often through the process of harming their metabolisms
with excessive carb consumption.**

How Dogs Get Fat

The Four-Stage Development of Canine Obesity

Overweight and obesity, in dogs as well as humans, usually develops over a period of several years. At any time during this period of years, the development can be stopped.

Many people seem to think, "Weight management is simple. It consists of just eating fewer calories than you burn with activity – whether it's people or dogs." That's not a simple explanation: It's a simplistic explanation. There's more to it than that. Weight control is never just a matter of calories eaten versus calories burned. That's part of it, but the other part is: what kind of calories you eat. This same principle applies to your dog.

For example, if you lived on an extremely high-carb diet composed exclusively of Coca Cola and Wonder Bread, you might be able to meet your basic nutritional needs, and survive. But would you be healthy? Would you be slender? No! Man does not live by bread and Coke alone.

If you tried to live on this diet, you would wreak havoc upon your metabolism. You wouldn't stay full and satisfied. You wouldn't get enough protein to feel good. And worst of all, you would almost certainly go through the four-stage metabolic decline that afflicts many people who eat excessive amounts of carbs. That four-stage progression is:

(1) *Hypoglycemia*. That's low blood sugar. It's very common – in people, and also in their pets, if the pets subsist mostly on high-grain foods.

(2) *Hyperglycemia*. This is high blood sugar. It comes next, after the body starts to break down. The body just can't move enough sugar into the cells.

(3) *Syndrome X*. This is the stage in which you, or your dog, really start to feel run-down. It is sometimes called "prediabetes."

(4) *Diabetes*. This is the last stop on the train of overweight and obesity. About 90% of all humans and animals with diabetes are overweight or obese.

This four-stage progression was once relatively uncommon, especially in animals. In the days when most dogs ran freely outside and did not live primarily on grain, these problems were seen primarily just in very old dogs. Not any longer. Now this phenomenon is extremely common.

It's quite possible that your dog has already begun to go down this four-stage road to disaster. Let's take a closer look at the stages, so you can start doing something about it now – before it's too late.

The First Stage of Dangerous Canine Obesity

Carbohydrates, which can be either starch or sugar, are one of the three basic categories of foods, along with protein and fat. Unlike protein and fat, though, which contain components your dog uses to rebuild himself (such as amino acids and fatty acids), carbs have only one function. They serve as fuel. That's it. Starch and sugar provide nothing else.

They are the canine body's front-line source of fuel because they are so chemically similar to blood sugar, or glucose. It takes almost no effort for a dog's body to produce glucose from various sugars, such as sucrose (table sugar), or lactose (milk sugar). These sugars sprint right into your system. Surprisingly, though, the calories from refined starch often hit the system as quickly as those from pure sugar, because the canine body, just like the human body, turns starch into sugar almost immediately.

These carb calories smash into your dog's system like a flash-flood, triggering a reaction that initially feels good. Blood sugar rockets, creating the famous "sugar rush," which really should be called a "carb rush," since refined starch is just as potent as sugar.

Sadly, people and their dogs pay an exorbitant price for this ephemeral high: a long-lasting rebound low that makes them feel weak, hungry, and irritable. Most people, and many dogs, suffer this distress frequently. Any time they eat too many carbs – which happens often, in our society – they soon suffer an energy slump, and often overeat to compensate for it.

For a huge segment of the human population, and an indeterminant portion of the dog population, this problem is devastating. It occurs so often, and with so much intensity, that many people, and many pets, are considered to be "carbohydrate intolerant." For them, carbs are almost like a drug, one they just can't handle.

When dogs who become carbohydrate intolerant eat too many carbs, it causes wild fluctuations in their levels of the hormone insulin, which moves blood sugar out of the bloodstream and into the cells, where it provides energy. A meal that's heavy in carbs can cause insulin to increase tenfold in just minutes. These insulin swings are a disaster, because they cause energy swings.

When insulin is stable, blood sugar flows into cells at a steady rate, and dogs tend to feel good: energetic, and not hungry. When dogs eat too many carbs, though, they jump on a roller coaster of energy highs and lows.

The first stage of this insulin instability is known as hypoglycemia, or low blood sugar. Hypoglycemia not only affects how your dog feels, but also how your dog eats. It makes dogs tend to eat too much. Then, when they overeat, the extra food only solves the problem temporarily – and then makes it even worse. The starch blocker strategy is perfect for helping end obesity due to carbohydrate and insulin problems. By flattening the curve of carb-calorie consumption, it can stop the four-stage spiral of high-carb weight gain before it ever gets started.

Hypoglycemia is often just the very beginning of dogs' problems with carbohydrates. Left unchecked, hypoglycemia gradually progresses to the next stage in the spiral of carb-related weight gain: hyperglycemia, or high blood sugar.

The Second Stage of Dangerous Canine Obesity

The second stage is hyperglycemia. Hyperglycemia is horrible. Having it is almost like having permanent hypoglycemia. People suffer terribly from it, and dogs do, too.

Hyperglycemia starts after dogs chronically overeat carbs and overproduce insulin for a long period of time. This chronic overproduction not only depletes their supplies of insulin, but it also causes their cells to become resistant to the actions of insulin. The cells develop tolerance to insulin, in somewhat the same way that the cells of heroin addicts develop tolerance to opiates, requiring ever higher amounts.

Hyperglycemia eventually strikes up to an estimated 25% of all people, generally as they approach midlife, and is a crucial factor in the human epidemic of overweight. No one is sure how common hyperglycemia is among dogs, because its symptoms are often subjective, rather than objective symptoms that can be measured. Judging by its prevalence in the human population, though, hyperglycemia may affect up to 25% of all overweight dogs, particularly if they are old, and have been living on a high-carb diet for many years.

When hyperglycemia occurs, too much blood sugar just sits sluggishly in the bloodstream, as cells literally begin to starve. These cells send out distress signals, interpreted by your dog's brain as hunger and irritation. As a rule, dogs want to get rid of these feelings by eating, but that only solves the problem partially and temporarily. Even with these temporary corrections, though, your dog's body and brain are still temporarily deprived of adequate blood sugar, causing widespread damage and death to cells.

It might seem as if things can't get much worse. But they can. Syndrome X can strike.

The Third Stage of Dangerous Canine Obesity

Syndrome X is a recently discovered condition in humans. In all probability, it is also prevalent among dogs, although this has not been scientifically proven. It is harder to prove the subjective symptoms of Syndrome X than it is to prove the existence of a frank disease state, such as diabetes, which typically follows Syndrome X. It's safe to say, though, that when diabetes occurs, Syndrome X probably preceded it.

Syndrome X hits when hyperglycemia combines with carbohydrate intolerance, insulin resistance, high levels of blood fats, and excess body fat. This dangerous combination of factors comes together in approximately 20% of all middle-aged people and makes weight loss almost impossible for them. Any one of these factors is terribly disruptive to normal metabolism, but when they gang together, they overwhelm the body. They keep blood sugar out of the cells, including the brain cells, to a dangerous degree. The only way to temporarily relieve Syndrome X symptoms is to overeat, and literally force blood sugar into cells, but this just makes the problem worse in the long run.

Not recognized until 1988, Syndrome X is now considered one of the largest epidemics ever to befall the American human population, according to a recent article in the Journal of the American Medical Association.

Like the conditions that lead to it, Syndrome X, in dogs, as well as humans, is badly exacerbated by eating too many carbohydrates, which is, unfortunately, exactly what people and dogs tend to do in order to fight the noxious symptoms of the problem. It's like throwing fuel on a fire. Even when the various factors composing Syndrome X do not become severe, they can still combine to become a major cause of weight gain in dogs.

This condition kills cells throughout the canine body and brain and is a major precursor of many degenerative diseases, including cardiovascular disease, cancer, and Alzheimer's (which strikes dogs, as well as people). It is most closely linked, though, to the final step in the degenerative spiral of canine, carb-related weight gain: diabetes.

The Last Stage of Dangerous Canine Obesity

About 13% of the U.S. human population has diabetes, and more than one-third of them don't even realize it. The incidence in the canine population is believed to be lower, in part because many dogs with diabetes are euthanized. Even so, diabetes has become increasingly common among dogs.

In some dogs, the disease is controlled carefully by limiting intake of carbohydrates to a spartan degree. When this is done, it helps reduce symptoms of the disease. Obviously, though, this degree of food denial to a dog can be a terrible burden, on the dog and its guardian. It's so difficult that many people just can't manage it, and their companion animals often suffer horrendous consequences. Blindness. Amputations. Kidney failure. Nerve disease. Death.

Diabetes, in our current era of high-carb intake, is more common among humans than ever, and it is striking ever younger people even children. In fact, diabetes is now so prevalent among kids that the name of the obesity-related type of the disease has been changed from Adult Onset diabetes to Type II diabetes. Among dogs, there has been a strikingly similar increase in incidence of the disease, probably due to their increased carb consumption.

Starch blockers offer great promise even to people, and dogs, with well-established diabetes. This was demonstrated in studies at Mayo Clinic and in Japan. These studies indicated that starch blockers may be able to allow people and dogs with diabetes to enjoy much more normal eating patterns while actually reducing the degree of their complications from diabetes.

The implications of this are astonishing. It probably represents the most important advance against diabetes since the introduction of insulin treatment. Perhaps even more momentous is the realistic possibility that starch blockers may help prevent the onset of human and canine diabetes. If widespread prevention of this killer occurs and we firmly believe it can this organic substance will become entrenched as one of veterinary medicine's most important new protocols.

Failure of the Current Approaches to Canine Obesity

As you probably know, among humans, a legion of insulin-stabilizing weight control programs has already been created to try to stop this four-stage progression. Each has been announced with great fanfare, each touting a twist: reliance on protein, reliance on fat, on strenuous exercise, on pharmaceutical drugs, and on appetite suppressants.

But each has failed for the majority of people trying it.

Similarly, many approaches have been applied to canine obesity.

The most common approach to helping dogs slim down is simply to limit their food intake. Sounds easy enough. But try it! Many dogs simply will not tolerate food restriction – especially if their metabolisms have already been harmed by excessive carb intake. The ravages of hypoglycemia, hyperglycemia, Syndrome X, and diabetes can transform well-behaved dogs into food-crazy rascals! These metabolic problems can make people – who are generally intelligent and well-educated – make poor food choices. Needless to say, the impact of these forces upon dogs is even more profound. Dogs don't understand why they're hungry. They only know they're dying to eat something, and will beg, whine, and bark until they get it. Can you blame them?

The second most popular method of canine weight management is use of reduced-calorie dog foods. For the most part, these are dry foods that have extra amounts of indigestible fibers added to them. Sometimes fat content is also reduced. This approach has been effective for many dogs, but can have drawbacks. The most common drawback is that some of these dog foods do not really satisfy a dog's hunger. They provide bulk, but pass through the system rather quickly. Also, these low-calorie dog foods have relatively fewer nutrients per pound than regular dog foods. Some of these nutrients – such as chromium, for example – appear to help control hunger, by stabilizing blood sugar levels.

Another drawback of some of the high-fiber dog foods is that they cause increased stool volume, and can contribute to flatulence. In some cases, this digestive disruption makes dogs uncomfortable.

Another approach to canine weight control is the use of herbal weight remedies for dogs, but most of them are scientifically unproven. We don't recommend them. The fact is, no approach introduced until now has been able to adequately address the resistant condition of canine obesity.

If any approach to canine obesity had proven effective, there would be no epidemic of obesity.

Finally, though, there's a new way to fight canine obesity – with the starch blocker strategy.

The starch blocker strategy to canine weight management is wholly different from all other approaches, because it allows dogs to eat normal foods in normal amounts, and still lose weight. This keeps dogs – and their guardians – happy.

There are, in fact, five major differences that set this weight management strategy apart from others. these five differences apply to the humans who have employed the starch blocker strategy, and they apply to dogs, too.

Your Dog Will Notice the Difference

Here are the major differences in the starch blocker strategy, in order of importance.

1. **This is the first canine non-denial weight program.**
   - Your dog can eat a normal amount of food, without assimilating all the calories.
   - Eliminating starch calories allows for consumption of relatively more calories from proteins, fats, and sugars.
   - Your dog can eat the types of foods he or she likes, instead of "lite," diet foods.

2. **This is the first no-hunger weight program.**
   - Abdominal fullness, caused by calorie-neutralized starchy foods, activates the "stretch receptors" in your dog's stomach that help switch off physical hunger.
   - Insulin stability, achieved by blocking starch calories, stops blood sugar and insulin swings, and the hunger that they cause.
   - Being able to freely enjoy food – and to add some non-starch calories – eliminates the psychological element of hunger that bothers many dogs– that feeling of being deprived.

3. **This is the first weight program that safely directs your dog's body to burn stored fat.**
   - Unlike low-calorie diets, this new strategy doesn't break down muscle tissue by restricting protein, and it doesn't starve the body of other necessary nutrients.

- Unlike conventional low-carbohydrate diets, it doesn't call for abundant consumption of high-fat foods, which can hurt your dog's health.

- Unlike low-fat diets, it doesn't call for high intake of carbohydrates, which can disrupt your dog's insulin stability.

- This approach makes exercise burn your dog's body fat more efficiently. It supercharges exercise by reducing stored carbohydrates, which your dog's body must deplete before it can burn body fat.

4. **This is the first weight management approach that appears capable of relieving complications from canine diabetes.**

- This strategy can help to arrest some of the symptoms of diabetes in dogs.

- This strategy has been shown to control the canine precursor conditions of diabetes, including hypoglycemia, hyperglycemia, and Syndrome X.

5. **This weight management strategy has no side effects.**

- It doesn't employ general stimulants, metabolic stimulants, or appetite suppressants.

- It doesn't raise your dog's cholesterol or other blood fats.

- It doesn't destabilize your dog's insulin levels.

- It has been certified 100% free of physical side effects by researchers employed by the National Institutes of Health.

- It doesn't contribute to a sense of deprivation.

This is the Future

It represents the future of weight management in companion animals, just as it represents the future of weight control in humans.

There has never before been anything remotely like this.

It's effective.

It's safe.

It's affordable.

And it's practical.

Consider trying it. If you don't, as the next chapter shows, you may eventually be forced to consider the alternatives: alternatives that can be heartbreaking.

Chapter Three

Don't Let This Happen To The Dog You Love

You'll Learn:

- Why so many canine diseases are related to obesity.
- Why obesity-related diseases are on the rise.
- Why diabetes is killing so many dogs.

- **How you can prevent these problems from ever starting.**

Pono arrived panting and breathless at the veterinary clinic of Dr. Curtis Willauer, one of the first veterinarians in America to treat dogs with starch blockers.

Dr. Willauer was alarmed at Pono's condition. Pono's breath was coming in short, raspy grunts, almost as if he were suffocating. In a sense, he was suffocating beneath layers of fat. To Dr. Willauer, Pono looked like an overstuffed loaf of bread. For the prior 10 years, the dog had gradually been gaining weight. Pono's guardian had tried to help him lose weight, first by restricting his feedings, and then by switching him to a special weight-control dog food. But nothing had worked. The weight had just kept piling on.

Now the extra weight was striking at Pono's particular point of vulnerability, as obesity always does. For example, in large dogs that are prone to dysplasia, obesity often exploits existing joint problems. Pono had some digestive problems, but his primary vulnerability was his ability to breathe. Pono was a Pug, a breed that is typically prone to breathing problems. Pugs have shortened, or stenotic, nostrils, and excessively long soft palates, which tends to compromise their breathing, even when they are healthy. When they become overweight, these natural vulnerabilities are exacerbated. Pono's extra weight was making him miserable, and was a potentially potent threat to his health, because breathing problems often stress the cardiovascular system.

Dr. Willauer did a full work-up on Pono, including a serum chemistry profile, urine analysis, and radiographic studies. The tests revealed that Pono's general metabolism had already begun to suffer, due to his respiratory distress. Instead of trying to change Pono's diet – an approach that had already failed – Dr. Willauer prescribed starch blockers.

During Pono's first week on starch blockers, his digestion began to improve. For some time, Pono had suffered from indigestion and bloating, and these symptoms suddenly began to disappear. This improvement seemed to indicate that Pono had probably been reactive to the high amounts of carbohydrates in his diet, or to the large volume of fiber from the weight-control dog food he'd been eating.

Pono's weight began to drop off. In a matter of weeks, Pono was significantly slimmer. Predictably, his breathing improved, and his stamina increased. Pono was soon his old self again. His guardian was delighted. Dr. Willauer was excited.

Another dog – probably headed for disease – had been saved.

Obesity is among the most harmful of all physical conditions for dogs. It contributes to most of the diseases that kill them.

The Dire Consequences of Canine Obesity

Dogs just don't thrive when they're overweight. Sometimes obesity limits their quality of life – and sometimes it limits life itself.

Here are some of the major problems that are directly associated with canine obesity.

DIABETES

This is the disease that is most closely associated with obesity. If you can keep your companion animal from becoming obese, you can limit its vulnerability to diabetes by an estimated 90%.

If your dog is drinking much more water than previously, for no apparent reason, or has experienced unexplained weight loss, it is quite possible that he or she has diabetes. Other signs of the disease are poor condition of the skin or coat, liver dysfunction, vomiting, weakness in the rear legs, proneness to dehydration, frequency of bacterial infections, or eyesight problems. Some of these signs, unfortunately, reflect advanced diabetes. The early stage of the disease is often difficult to ascertain in dogs, because many of its symptoms are subjective. In fact, early-stage diabetes is even hard to ascertain among humans. About one-third of the people who have diabetes don't know it.

Diabetes is significantly more common now in dogs than it once was, probably for the same reasons it's now more common among humans: because of the obesity epidemic, and because of diets that are too high in fast-burning carbs. An estimated 1.5 of every 100 dogs has diabetes. Female dogs are about twice as likely as males to suffer from it.

This degree of incidence may, however, be quite understated, because, as we mentioned, it can be very difficult to diagnose early-stage diabetes in dogs, and because late-state diabetic dogs are often euthanized.

To diagnose diabetes, a veterinarian will run a number of blood and urine tests. The urine will be checked for its degree of concentration, for its level of blood sugar, and for the presence of blood and certain amino acids, such as creatine. The normal blood glucose level in dogs is between 60 and 120. If an abnormally high glucose level is found, dogs will generally be kept at a clinic or hospital for several days as other tests are performed.

When a positive diagnosis is made, many pet owners face the terrible decision of euthanasia. It can be difficult and expensive to treat dogs with diabetes, and there is no cure for the disease. This is a disease that dog guardians should focus on preventing, rather than treating.

The best ways to prevent it are to keep blood sugar levels stable, with the help of starch blockers, and to avoid obesity.

JOINT DISORDERS

These problems are also very closely related to obesity. Obesity is often not the direct cause of the joint disorders, but severely aggravates them, just as obesity aggravates human joint problems, such as arthritis.

Arthritis is also relatively common in dogs, particularly if they are older. In almost all cases, arthritis pain in obese dogs can be reduced if the dogs lose weight. Arthritis can also be treated in dogs with some of the same natural substances that can be helpful for human arthritis, such as glucosamine, chondroitin, creatine, MSM, and such anti-inflammatory agents as omega-3 fatty acids and low doses of aspirin.

These same substances can also be helpful, especially in mild cases, for one of the worst joint diseases in dogs is hip dysplasia. Hip dysplasia is a genetic disease, not caused by overweight. However, extra pounds can make it far more painful, by stressing the hip joint.

Similarly, many dogs also suffer from elbow dysplasia, a hereditary disease in which the elbow joints are malformed. Surgery and anti-inflammatories can improve the condition, but surgery can be very expensive, and sometimes triggers onset of arthritis. For overweight dogs, weight reduction generally reduces the pain from this condition. Another joint condition that is made more painful by excess weight is OCD, or osteochondrosis dissecans. This is a thickening of the cartilage in the joint areas. Thickened cartilage is prone to damage, often resulting in a noticeable limp, especially after strenuous activity.

There are also certain musculoskeletal injuries that are directly caused by carrying excess weight. One example is cruciate ligament injury, a problem that is similar to the same type of injury that athletes often suffer. This injury strikes dogs' stifle joints, which are equivalent to the human knee joints. In many cases, this problem could have been avoided entirely by maintaining proper weight. As you can see, many joint and connective tissue disorders occur in dogs, and occur more often in purebreds than mixed breeds.

Obesity makes every one of these problems more painful.

CANCER

Cancer is the number-one disease killer of dogs, and is often associated with obesity. Dogs that are 10 years old, or older, have an approximately 50% chance of contracting cancer.

Some canine cancers, such as bladder cancer, have a clear link to obesity, but in other cancers, the link is less well established.

The link between obesity and cancer has been studied far more in humans than in dogs, and the human findings are quite possibly applicable to dogs. There are some notable exceptions, though. For example, colon cancer is one of the most common types of cancer in humans, and has a 12% association rate with obesity, but colon cancer is still relatively uncommon among dogs.

In humans, the link between obesity and cancer is alarmingly high. Cancers linked to obesity among women comprised 51% of all new cancers in 2002, according to the American Cancer Society, and obesity was associated with 14% of all new cancers among men.

Unfortunately, for dogs, one of the clearest links between cancer and obesity in humans is for breast cancer – which is the most common form of cancer in dogs, accounting for an estimated 51% of all female canine cancers. In humans, there is a 31% association rate between breast cancer and obesity. In dogs, breast cancer is twice as common among purebreds as mixed breeds. Breast cancer occasionally occurs in male dogs, but 97% of it is found in females.

Extrapolating from the human figures – which is admittedly an inexact science – it makes common sense for guardians of female purebreds to be wary of obesity in their dogs. Spaying female dogs confers some protection against this type of cancer, but only if it is done before the dog is 2-1/2 years old, and preferably before the dog's first heat.

In humans, it has long been suspected, but never unequivocally proven, that excess dietary fat increases incidence of breast cancer. In dogs, however, studies seem to indicate that excess fat is not a specific contributory factor. The primary contributory factor appears simply to be excess weight – regardless of what caused this weight.

Obesity can also make existing canine breast cancer worse. One study showed that obese dogs with breast cancer were four times as likely as normal-weight dogs with breast cancer to have aggressive, fast-growing tumors. The evidence is clear: Obesity contributes to canine cancer. The smart approach is to stop this problem before it starts.

CARDIOVASCULAR DISEASE

Dr. Barry Sears, creator of The Zone Diet, was one of the pioneers of the low-carb approach to weight management and health. In his studies, he found that there were many similarities between canine and human physiology. Because of this, he created a Canine Zone Diet, a low-carb dog food product which appears to be one of the more effective nutritional approaches to canine obesity. He found, in particular, that a carb-controlled diet was notably effective for helping to prevent cardiovascular disease in dogs.

As Dr. Sears' associate, Stephanie Kress, has noted, heart disease is relatively common in dogs. While some dogs are born with developmental heart problems, most develop their problems during adulthood or old age, often because of how much they eat, and what they eat.

In most cases, heart disease can be successfully managed by early detection and treatment. Weight reduction and a carb-control strategy appear to help a great deal.

Of the dogs in the United States examined annually by veterinarians, approximately 3.2 million have some form of heart disease, and many are in heart failure. Canine heart failure results from the heart's inability to pump blood at a rate required to meet the needs of the dog's body. While the heart continues to work harder to pump blood, further damage can occur.

The most common congenital cardiovascular problem among dogs is patent ductus arteriosus, or PDA. When this heart duct doesn't close as it should, blood is pushed back through the heart, instead of throughout the body. This can cause exercise intolerance, increased breathing rate, and coughing or collapsing during exercise.

Congestive heart failure is the most severe form of heart disease for a dog, and it occurs when the heart weakens, and can no longer pump effectively. Some dogs with heart failure are classic couch potatoes – overweight and inactive. Obesity can harm your dog's heart in many ways. It can directly cause cardiovascular problems, and can turn a mild heart problem into a more serious one.

Dogs also often suffer from blood vessel diseases, just as humans do. For many years, it was believed that excessive dietary fat was by far the greatest contributor to the build-up of cholesterol and other obstructive factors in blood vessels. More recently, though, it has become clear that any dietary factor that increases body fat contributes to the increase of fat in the blood. Carbs, for example, can be quickly transformed into body fat, and fat in the bloodstream.

The evidence is overwhelming: *Your dog needs to have a healthy weight, and a healthy diet, in order to have a healthy heart.*

LIVER AND PANCREATIC DISEASES

Liver disease is relatively common in dogs, and can be exacerbated by obesity.

Hepatitis, or inflammation of the liver, is the most common liver disease among dogs, developing most often in animals at least 6 to 8 years of age. It affects all breeds, but Dobermans are somewhat more susceptible. About two-thirds of the time, the cause is unknown, but is generally believed to be a virus, a drug, or an immune response. In the other one-third of cases, it's usually caused by infection, cancer, gastrointestinal disease, or kidney disease.

Extrapolating from human data, hepatitis, which is often fatal, can be exacerbated in dogs by obesity.

Another common liver ailment, fatty liver, is also associated with obesity.

But the liver, among all other organs, has a unique capacity for regeneration, and liver diseases can frequently be cured with healthy lifestyle factors, such as detoxification, and removal of contributory factors, including obesity. Liver diseases in dogs can be very hard to diagnose. Often, the only certain diagnosis comes from a liver biopsy. By the time this extreme measure is taken, it is often too late to save the dog's life. Almost one-third of all dogs diagnosed with hepatitis die in a matter of weeks. Like virtually all other serious conditions, liver diseases are easier to prevent than to cure.

The most common pancreatic disease in dogs is inflammation of the pancreas, or pancreatitis. Pancreatitis has a notable association with obesity. The pancreas is the site of production of pancreatic digestive enzymes, so it is possible that the pancreas could become stressed merely by having to produce excessive digestive enzymes, in response to consumption of large amounts of food, and could become diseased in reaction to this ongoing stressor.

HEAT INTOLERANCE AND SKIN PROBLEMS

It's just common sense: If a dog is swathed in extra layers of fat, the animal will often be too warm. Being covered by all that fat is almost like having to wear an extra overcoat. Therefore, overweight dogs are much more prone to heat intolerance. This heat intolerance can contribute to the development of hot spots, which are areas of skin inflammation, or moist dermatitis. These hot spots often become infected. They can be very painful, and hard to cure. The area around them may need to be shaved, and the dogs may need to be treated with corticosteroids and antibiotics.

Also, obese dogs often have trouble grooming themselves. When rolls of fat build up, they can harbor dirt, bacteria, and other organisms.

This harm to your dog's skin is one final reason to keep your dog slim and healthy. Being fat feels bad, minute after minute, day after day, year after day.

All of these many problems, plus the physical stress of obesity itself, significantly shortens the lives of obese dogs. Disorders that are related to obesity are the fourth leading cause of death among dogs, according to the American Veterinary Medical Association.

A recent study showed that decreasing caloric intake of dogs can increase longevity by 15%. In this study, a group of Labrador retrievers was fed 25% fewer calories than labs in a control group, and lived an average of 13 years, compared to 11 years among the control group. The leaner dogs had less cancer, arthritis, and liver disease. They also had an apparently superior quality of life. They were friskier and looked younger and fitter than the dogs that had eaten more.

Obviously, obesity is a terrible health problem for dogs.

- It makes them miserable.
- It makes them sick.
- It kills them.

But this doesn't have to happen.

Starch blockers can help keep it from happening.

We know this. And we want you to know it – not just because we say so, but because solid scientific evidence has proven it. In the next chapter, we'll tell you about the scientific history of starch blockers, and about the studies that support their use. Then you can decide for yourself what's best for your dog.

Chapter Four

How We
Know This
Works

You'll Learn:

- How Howard Hughes helped discover starch blockers.
- How Mayo Clinic proved they work.
- How they were tested throughout the world.

- **How the type of starch blocker known as Phase 2™
  can reverse your dog's obesity!**

The Howard Hughes Connection

Starch blockers were first developed under the direction of the legendary Howard Hughes. In his declining years, the billionaire was best known for his eccentricities, including reclusiveness and an extreme phobia of germs. Before that, though, he was widely recognized as an extraordinary engineering innovator, a keen observer of new sciences, and an ardent supporter of medical research. His group of Howard Hughes Medical Institutes is still one of the finest consortiums of research hospitals in the world.

In 1971, Howard Hughes, or one of his top aides, spotted an article in an obscure scientific journal that would eventually change the direction of weight management, for humans as well as animals. The article described a mystery.

For reasons unknown, mice in an experiment that had been conducted in Venezuela had died of starvation, even though they'd been fed a seemingly nutritious diet. The article said that perhaps some form of "antinutrient" had caused the baffling starvation. Hughes assigned a team of researchers at Miami's Howard Hughes Medical Institute to look into the mystery. The group was headed by George Thorn, the hospital's director of medical research. Over the next two years Thorn's research team linked the Venezuelan mystery to existing knowledge about certain antinutrient proteins that inhibit food digestion by binding with the digestive enzymes of insects, animals, and human beings.

It has been known since the 1940s, for example, that raw, unprocessed wheat contains small amounts of a protein that binds with the receptor sites on alpha amylase, the enzyme that digests starch. This makes the amylase temporarily incapable of breaking down starch. The protein stays in the system – "stuck" to the enzyme – for only about an hour. It's quickly moved through the digestive tract, along with the enzyme and the other food substances that were eaten, and is excreted.

While it is in the system, though, it renders amylase incapable of breaking down all of the starch that's present. This undigested starch then passes through the system in whole-molecule form, with the other foodstuffs. Because the undigested starch stays in whole-molecule form, it does not release any calories.

This enzyme-inhibiting protein helps protect wheat in the field and in storage bins. When insects and animals, such as weevils and mice, scavenge raw wheat, they ingest this protein, which prohibits digestion of some of the starch from the wheat. This discourages insects and animals from eating raw wheat. When they try to live on it, they don't get enough calories, so they tend to abandon it. Thus, enzyme inhibitors are protective mechanisms born of evolution that enable plants to survive, much the same way that the spines on a cactus or the thorns on a blackberry vine help those plants to survive.

What researchers discovered at the Howard Hughes Medical Institute – and in related research at the University of Miami – was that the plants with the most abundant amounts of this enzyme-inhibiting antinutrient were white beans. And white beans had primarily composed the diet of the Venezuelan mice that had starved to death. End of mystery. Solving the mystery of the starving mice was just the beginning. Then the real work started.

The researchers named the enzyme-inhibiting substance in white beans "phaseolamin." The word is derived from the Latin word for kidney beans, phaseo vulgaris, combined with am (short for "amylase") and in (short for "inhibitor").

Even today, some medical experts incorrectly assume that phaseolamin is a compound, but it's just a vegetable glycoprotein with a very specific molecular weight. In effect, it's a part of a part of a part of a specific plant protein.

The initial interest in phaseolamin among almost all researchers was as a tool to fight diabetes. Researchers were well aware that eating excessive amounts of starch can be critically injurious to people with diabetes, because it rushes glucose into the bloodstream. They hoped phaseolamin would help curtail this rush.

For several years, during the latter 1970s, they worked on isolating phaseolamin from other substances in white beans, especially "lectins," which can cause blood cells to clump together. The researchers were, in a sense, trying to find a standardized, replicable way to pull the "needle" of phaseolamin out of the "haystack" of white beans.

This refinement process was exceptionally difficult. It was easy to just grind up beans, but that left in too many impurities. Ground-up beans did seem to have a moderate enzyme-inhibiting action, but they caused too many side effects, such as bloating and diarrhea.

Unfortunately, this did not stop some of the people who had been researching starch blockers from rushing them to market. In 1982, crude bean extracts began to appear on the market and were sold for weight loss. Sales of these products were strong, and for several months these crude "starch blockers" became a new fad. A couple of reputable laboratories joined the effort, and did manage to produce pure starch blockers that were generally effective, although expensive. However, the market was dominated by the cheaper, impure, ineffective products, which were markedly inferior to today's vastly improved version of the product.

The Food and Drug Administration quickly intervened. They ruled that it wasn't legal for retailers to claim that all of these "starch blockers" caused weight loss. To do so would be a health claim, and at that time, the only products that could make health claims were drugs.

When retailers could no longer sell starch blockers explicitly for weight control, almost all American companies lost interest in the approach. For them, it was like trying to sell Diet Pepsi without being able to mention that it was calorie-free. However, two companies that had adequate refining processes did continue to market them, without any promotion, and they remained moderately popular in a few other countries, including Italy.

In 1983, the *Journal of The American Medical Association* published a study in which researchers tested the effectiveness of several of the most popular, old, crude bean extract products that had been sold for weight loss. Predictably, they exerted only a minimal degree of enzyme inhibition, which resulted in negligible weight loss. The article concluded, quite accurately, that these crude bean extracts were not efficacious. When that article appeared, most of the research community lost interest in starch blockers.

The Mayo Clinic Goes To Work

Not Mayo Clinic, though. Doctors there, led by Eugene P. DiMagno, M.D., continued to investigate the potential of starch blockers for helping diabetics. Unlike most other researchers at that time, they did not accept at face value the conclusion of the JAMA article that starch blockers were necessarily ineffective. Prior research clearly showed that starch blockers were effective in test-tube experiments, or "in vitro." As a general rule, if actions occur in vitro, they will also probably occur within the human and animal bodies, or "in vivo." Therefore, Dr. DiMagno and his associates continued the research that had begun at the Howard Hughes Medical Institute, looking for ways to improve the extraction process. They needed to increase the amount of active starch-inhibition material in each dosage, and to eliminate all possible contaminants.

Major advances were made. A pure, much more active product was produced. In 1984, Dr. DiMagno, along with Drs. Peter Layer and Gerald Carlson, tested this new version of starch blockers against some of the old commercial formulas, and against crude bean extracts. The new Mayo Clinic formula was vastly more effective and proved quite capable in test tubes of inhibiting starch breakdown by human amylase.

This was the beginning of 15 years of starch blocker research by Mayo Clinic. Between 1984 and 1999, researchers there completed 13 studies and published all of them in peer-reviewed medical or scientific journals, including the *New England Journal of Medicine, Gastroenterology,* the Mayo *Clinic Proceedings, Pancreas, and Nutrition.*

Most of these studies involved dogs.

The research of Dr. DiMagno and his colleagues laid the groundwork for all future investigation of starch blockers and became the "gold standard" against which later research was measured. Among the Mayo Clinic researchers' most significant determinations was, "We conclude that a purified amylase inhibitor is effective, and potentially beneficial in the treatment of diabetes mellitus."

Most of the Mayo Clinic research was aimed at investigating the use of starch blockers not against obesity but against diabetes. All of the results were promising.   None of the research was definitive, however, as is generally the case when a new substance is tested against a deadly disease. The Mayo Clinic studies also tested the viability of wheat amylase inhibitors, but found that they were not strong enough to be effective in humans.

The Mayo Clinic did do a small amount of research on weight loss, and found, not surprisingly, that because starch blockers inhibited starch digestion, they were also effective, in animal experiments, as a weight loss aid. The Mayo Clinic studies gradually reignited interest in starch blockers among other members of the international biological research community, particularly in Japan. From 1992 until 2001, 11 separate studies were conducted at Kyushu University, Hokkaido University of Sapporo, Osaka University, and at other Japanese universities and medical institutions. All were published in peer-reviewed, international medical journals.

Among the findings:

- Use of starch blockers heightened glucose stability in humans and dogs, and reduced episodes of hypoglycemia.

- Starch blockers suppressed elevation of blood glucose immediately after people or animals ate starch, thereby reducing triglycerides, free fatty acids, and total cholesterol.

- Starch blockers ameliorated various diabetes syndrome symptoms.

- Starch blockers create extra production of a substance called 3-hydroxybutyric acid, which has been shown in other studies to kill colon cancer cells.

The Mayo Clinic work was aimed at researching starch blocker use among humans. But Mayo Clinic used dogs in its testing. Therefore, much of the canine research has already been done.

Much of the Japanese research was aimed at improving the extraction methods for starch blockers. This research attracted virtually no interest from the general public, because it offered no immediate, practical application. However, it had a strong impact on the scientific community. As refinements were made in the process, starch blockers became increasingly effective and more financially feasible for commercial production. New studies on improved extraction methods proliferated around the world. Among the institutions that became involved were the University of California at San Diego, the University of Illinois, Canada's Institute for Biological Sciences, Brazil's University of Ponta Grossa, Northern Illinois University, and universities in Germany, France, and Scotland.

Despite this, major problems remained. By the mid-1990s, no institution had developed a refinement process that could deliver a highly potent version of starch blockers to the market at a price that most people could afford.

These problems were eventually solved by Pharmachem Laboratories of New Jersey. One of America's largest producers of bulk supplement products, this company is widely known for its emphasis on quality and purity and for its innovative techniques. At Pharmachem, Mitchell Skop, a research director and product developer, recognized the potential of starch blockers as a future weapon against diabetes, but also saw their immediate value as a weight management aid. Although this application seems stunningly obvious, particularly in light of starch blockers' brief but dramatic popularity as a weight control aid in 1982, it had been shunted aside by many researchers, who were more absorbed by starch blockers' potential for defeating diabetes. This degree of focus – some would say myopia – is not uncommon in science, particularly as it is practiced in academia. In major academic institutions, practicality often falls by the wayside.

Skop assigned a group of scientists, headed by Dr. Dilip Chokshi, to begin work on making a more potent, concentrated, and stable formula, one that would pass intact into the small intestine, where almost all starch digestion occurs in humans, and where all starch digestion occurs in dogs. He also wanted to find ways to extract the formula using only purified water, and using only raw ingredients from non-genetically modified organisms that had been grown without pesticides and contained no heavy metals. In the language of laboratory production, the process had to be "durable," producing a substance that would survive in the digestive tract, and it had to be "reproducible," so that any other qualified laboratory in the world could produce it.

Solving the Biggest Problem

After several years, the biggest remaining problem was purity. It was difficult to remove 100% of the naturally occurring lectins in white beans, which cause mild digestive problems, such as bloating and gas. Eventually, the problem yielded to an elegantly simple solution: using smaller beans. It was discovered that the smallest of the white beans, which contain the highest concentrations of starch blocker in the plant kingdom, have much lower concentrations of lectins than larger beans.

By 2000, Skop's research team was satisfied with their formula. "What we had produced," Skop later remarked, "was so different from the original formulas that it was no longer phaseolamin. However, everyone in the field of biological science was accustomed to the term "phaseolamin," so we just extrapolated from the common nomenclature and called it 'Phaseolamin 2250,' or 'Phase 2™.'"

Phaseolamin 2250 was markedly stronger than Mayo Clinic's substance. It was more concentrated, more stable in the gastrointestinal tract, and was completely free of impurities.

Skop began to authorize testing of Phaseolamin 2250 (which we'll refer to hereinafter as Phase 2™, for the sake of simplicity), as a weight loss aid in clinical studies. The same formula - Phase 2™ - was also later used for canine weight management.

One of the first tests was for safety. This test was performed in two segments by Dr. Radha Maheshwari, a scientist employed by the federal government's National Institutes of Health, although it was performed at a private research laboratory rather than in NIH facilities. In the first segment of the test, 160 rats were fed Phase 2™ for 14 days, in varying dosages. The first group was fed 200 mg. of Phase 2™ for every 5 kg. of their body weight- a very high dosage, in human terms, or in canine terms. Four other groups were fed even higher amounts, with the fourth group receiving 25 times as much as the first group. The rats were monitored for adverse reactions, and after 14 days they were sacrificed. Their bodies were autopsied, their organs were examined, and their tissues were studied with electron microscopes. No abnormalities of any kind, nor any signs of toxicity, were discovered. In the next segment of the study, the rats were fed Phase 2™ for 90 days instead of 14. Then the procedures were repeated with the same positive results. From this, it was concluded that Phase 2™ was free of any toxic effects.

The next series of tests, performed at the University of Scranton, were double-blind, placebo-control studies that determined that Phase 2™ blocked starch digestion in human volunteers. Four studies were done – under the direction of Professor Joe A. Vinson, Ph.D., of the Department of Chemistry – that proved conclusively that starch blockers inhibit starch digestion in humans.

In the first two studies, two groups of subjects were fed four slices of bread, and were then measured for blood glucose levels. The subjects in one of the groups took 1,500 mg. of starch blockers with the bread, and the other group took placebos. The group of subjects that had taken starch blockers experienced a noticeable flattening of the glycemic curve. Their blood glucose time curve – reflecting the amount of starch calories entering the blood-stream –was an average of 57% lower than that of subjects taking the placebo. In a similar, subsequent trial, results were even better. Only 15% of the starch calories in the bread were absorbed.

In the third study, Dr. Vinson mixed powdered starch blocker into the mashed potatoes of a Hungry Man TV dinner containing steak, potatoes, green beans, mushrooms, gravy, and crumb cake. In this study, the dosage of starch blocker was reduced by one-half, to 750 mg. It resulted in the blockage of only 28% of starch calories, which led Dr. Vinson to conclude that success appeared to be, to some degree, dose dependent.   Dr. Vinson concluded that "an even more significant difference in starch absorption may occur if respondents are given a higher dose of Phase 2™."

In 2001, at approximately the same time as the University of Scranton's series of studies, another study at the University of Illinois confirmed the ability of starch blockers to neutralize starch calories. Amylase activity was reduced by 50% to 75%, prompting researchers to conclude,"These results indicate that amylase inhibitor is effective in reducing amylase activity in vivo, and supports the hypothesis that an amylase inhibitor may reduce or delay carbohydrate absorption and glucose absorption." Clearly, starch blockers could reduce starch calorie absorption. But could they help people, or other animals, reduce their levels of body fat? That question was answered by the remaining major studies, which dealt solely with weight loss.

The first of these studies was conducted in Norway by Parexel Medstat and was published in the *Journal of International Medical Research*. In a 12-week trial, 40 obese volunteers were randomly assigned administration of a starch blocker or a placebo. The subjects taking starch blockers were not required to adhere to a prudent diet, but they still averaged 7.4 pounds of weight loss, which was more than three times greater than the loss achieved by patients on placebo. Furthermore, it was determined that 85% of the weight loss in the starch blocker group was fat loss, rather than loss of muscle, which was a higher percentage than the norm.

The study was flawed in two ways, however. Subjects were mistakenly advised to take the starch blockers *after* meals, instead of before meals. This probably decreased the effectiveness of the starch blockers and may well have accounted for the fact that people in this study achieved less weight loss than people in subsequent studies. Furthermore, subjects were also given another weight management aid, *Garcinia cambogia*, which contains a substance, hydroxycitrate, that appears to be helpful as a diet aid. The liability of taking the starch blockers too late in the meal probably hurt results more than the hydroxycitrate helped. However, these two factors still appear to have undermined the reliability of the study.

The next major study, by Italy's Pharmaceutical Development and Service, was conducted more carefully and achieved better results. In this study, patients taking starch blockers lost an average of 3.9% of total body weight – or an average of 6.45 pounds – over 30 days, with no significant loss of muscle mass. This weight loss of approximately 1.5 pounds per week was composed almost solely of fat. This compared to a weight loss among patients on placebo of only one-half of 1% – about three-quarters of a pound for a 150-pound person over 30 days, or about one-sixth of a pound per week. In addition, the 30 patients taking starch blockers averaged, in just 30 days, a reduction of about 11% of all adipose tissue; a 3.44% reduction of waist measurement; a 1.39% reduction of hip circumference; and a 1.44% reduction of thigh circumference. Patients on the placebo achieved no significant reductions in body measurements.

In this study, patients were advised to take only one starch blocker tablet per day and were not encouraged to exercise. The patients were all at least 30 pounds overweight, were all healthy, and were age 20 to 45.

Afterwards, the chief researcher, Dr. R. Ballerini, concluded "The study demonstrated the real capability of the considered product to determine in vivo weight loss through mass reduction, via reduced absorption, of complex carbohydrates."

Every study concluded that starch blockers had a powerful effect on weight reduction.

The most well-conducted weight loss study to date, though, was performed in 2002 by Jay Udani, M.D., Director of the Integrative Medicine Program at Northridge Hospital (a UCLA affiliate).

In his study, 50 patients, all under age 50, with body mass indexes of 30 to 35 (indicating obesity), were given either 1,500 mg. of the Phase 2™ formula up to twice a day, or a placebo, to be ingested with starchy meals. The study was randomized and double-blind, and lasted for eight weeks. The subjects were advised to eat daily diets that contained a moderate amount of carbohydrates – up to 200 grams, or 800 calories. They were also advised to eat diets that were relatively low in fat and relatively high in fiber.

The primary factor the study examined was weight loss. The secondary factors were the impact of starch blockers on triglycerides and waist measurements. In addition, Dr. Udani monitored patients for a subjective sense of well-being.

The results were dramatic and compelling.

The most relevant finding in the study was that the patients taking starch blockers lost an average of approximately four pounds over the course of the study, compared to an average of one and one-half pounds lost by the patients on placebo. This is a difference of approximately 230%.

The amount of weight lost was less than that lost by subjects in the study by Dr. Ballerini, but this degree of variation is not unusual in studies such as these, in which subjects' caloric intake is self-determined and can vary greatly. Even though Dr. Udani recommended that his subjects eat a low-fat, high-fiber diet that was moderate in carbs, he had no control over their adherence to the guidelines. It is predictable in this kind of a study that many subjects will stray from the guidelines and not report their indulgences, perhaps because of embarrassment, or simply a lack of awareness of their caloric intake. However, this variance could be expected equally from both the starch blocker group and the placebo group, so a sensible way to accurately interpret the outcome is to primarily compare the results of the two groups. In this comparison, the starch blocker group obviously fared far better than the control group at losing weight.

The starch blocker group was also more successful at losing inches. By eight weeks, they had lost an average of slightly more than one and one-half inches from their waists, which was 40% more than the average of the control group.

Some of the most revealing data came from objective measurements of triglycerides. Blood levels of triglycerides went down dramatically among starch blocker users, averaging a drop of 26 mg. per deciliter. Among the control group, triglycerides stayed at the same general plateau, dropping only 7 mg. per deciliter. Thus, the starch blocker group had a 370% better reduction in triglycerides than the control group.

There was also a difference in how much better the starch blocker group felt, compared to the control group. This is critically important, because how people feel in a weight management program is arguably the best predictor of how well they will succeed. Even if they're doing well by objective measurements – losing weight and inches and lowering their blood fat levels – they still usually don't succeed in the long run unless they're also feeling good. The starch blocker group felt better. They experienced a trend toward improvement in energy, even though the starch blocker is not a stimulant. This is a primary factor in keeping weight from creeping back on. Virtually no one can endure an energy-draining diet forever.

Another revealing aspect of the study was the analysis of the top performers. Among the group of starch blocker users, the five leading weight losers lost 18 pounds, 17 pounds, 10.5 pounds, 7 pounds, and 6.5 pounds (a combined total of 59 pounds). Among the control group, the five leading weight losers lost 6 pounds, 6 pounds, 5 pounds, 4.5 pounds, and 3 pounds (a combined total of 24.5 pounds). "These are the results that are possible," Dr. Udani noted, "though not typical."

At the conclusion of this study, Dr. Udani was impressed. "Apparently, the starch blocker substance, when used with daily ingestion of up to 200 grams of carbohydrate, contributed to persistent and steady weight loss," he said. "It appears to have had an effect on carbohydrate management by the body, as indicated by the triglyceride indexes." These were very positive trends.

The Hawaii Canine Study

Although many of the Mayo Clinic studies on starch blockers used dogs as the research animals, the dogs were essentially surrogates for humans, since the focus of the Mayo Clinic work was primarily on human diabetes. However, in 2004, veterinarians in Hawaii conducted a study that was focused solely upon helping dogs lose weight.

The study was directed by two of this book's authors – Curtis Willauer, D.V.M., and Barbara Ota, M.S. – and by Annette Timmel, D.V.M. It was carried out in two different veterinary clinics, one in Maui, and one on the Big Island. A total of 20 dogs, of different breeds, were in the study, all of whom were overweight or obese.

After initial testing to determine that the dogs were healthy, except for being overweight, the dogs were administered starch blockers each day for eight weeks. The dogs that weighed less than 50 pounds were given a dosage of one 500 mg. capsule with each meal, and dogs weighing 50 pounds or more were given two 500 mg. capsules with each meal. The starch blocker was sprinkled out of the capsules onto the dogs' food at the beginnings of meals.

The capsules were composed of Phase 2™, the only starch blocker product that has been extensively tested for safety and effectiveness. The brand name of the Phase 2™ product was VetSlim.

Seventeen of the 20 dogs completed the study. Three of the dogs' owners removed their dogs from the study because of difficulties with transportation and time. The owners of the dogs were instructed to make no significant changes in their dogs' lifestyles. The dogs did not exercise more than they previously had, nor did they receive a different amount of food than previously. The only notable difference was their use of starch blockers.

Of the 17 dogs who completed the study, 15 – or 87% – lost weight. The average amount of weight loss among these 15 dogs was 3.01 pounds, or 4.61% of body weight per dog. Equating this to humans, a 4.61% loss of body weight would be a loss of about 72 pounds for a 160-pound person – or just under one pound per week.

Therefore, the weight loss experienced by dogs was somewhat better than that achieved by humans in most studies.

The dogs also consistently lost inches around their waists, which is a prime area for fat deposits among dogs, as well as humans. Of the 15 dogs who completed the study, 13 lost inches, and two remained the same. The average amount of inches lost in the abdomen was 1.44 inches. Even the dogs who failed to lose weight lost inches. This appears to indicate that these dogs shifted some of their body composition from body-fat to lean muscle mass.

The loss of approximately 5% of body weight was encouraging in terms of disease prevention, because it's been demonstrated that, among humans, a 5% weight loss confers significant added protection against degenerative diseases – particularly diabetes.

After the study, all of the dogs were tested for signs of toxic reactions to the starch blockers, but no toxicity was noted.

The veterinarians conducting the study were impressed and encouraged. They felt that the results could have been even better if the starch blockers had been given to the dogs about 15 to 30 minutes before mealtimes, instead of with meals, because use of starch blockers by humans has been shown to be more effective when they are taken before meals. The vets also believed that the results would have been better if they had given dogs weighing more than 80 pounds three 500 mg. capsules, instead of two.

Furthermore, it's quite likely that results would have been even better if the dogs' owners had changed their dogs' exercise and food

programs. However, these changes would have made it more difficult to determine the exact value of starch blocker usage.

Slow and Steady Weight Reduction Works Best, For Humans As Well As Dogs

"In my opinion," said Dr. Udani, "the ideal way to lose weight is
slowly and consistently, at the rate of approximately one-half to one
pound per week. People using this substance were able to
approximate that goal, while still eating a nutritious and well-balanced
diet, which included reasonable amounts of carbohydrates.

"The primary reason most people appear to be unable to lose
weight and maintain that weight loss over the long term," he said, "is
because of general dissatisfaction with weight management diets.
It's my opinion, though, that people will be able to stick with the
starch blocker weight management approach, and thereby be able to
lose a significant amount of weight and keep it off over an extended
period of time."

Dr. Udani did not recommend exercise to the people in his
study because he wanted to determine if use of starch blockers
alone resulted in weight loss. However, he has stated, "I believe that
if people do add a prudent regimen of exercise to this protocol, they
may be able to achieve a weight loss goal of approximately one
pound per week, and maintain this rate of weight loss as they work
toward their ideal goal weights."

The Future

It appears as if the future is bright for further research on starch
blockers. The obvious opportunity is for their use against diabetes.
However, starch blockers may also prove to be helpful in controlling
at least two types of cancer associated with the digestive tract.

The first is colon cancer. This type of cancer is still relatively
uncommon among dogs, but it does occur. It has long been known
that increased digestive fiber is very helpful for preventing colon
cancer. The presumed mechanism of action for this protection is

decreased bowel transit time for digested food. The longer digested food remains in the colon, the more damage it is believed to do. Starch blockers create an effect that is similar to the ingestion of dietary fiber. By causing starch to remain in whole-molecule form, starch blockers effectively increase the fibrous texture of starch. Thus, this bulking effect may prove to exert colon cancer benefits similar to those created by the bulking action of fiber.

In addition, there's a relatively new theory about why fiber helps prevent colon cancer. According to it, fiber helps by mildly increasing fermentation in the bowel, which produces the chemical butyric acid. Recently, it was discovered that butyric acid inhibits growth of colon cancer cells. It helps stop them from growing by regulating a substance called epidermal growth factor, and also by regulating estrogen receptors. Starch blockers also mildly increase fermentation in the bowel, increasing production of butyric acid. Theoretically, this increase in butyric acid may help control colon cancer cell growth.

Therefore, starch blockers may one day prove to be a helpful ally against colon cancer.

Another promising benefit that may come from starch blockers is help in preventing pancreatic cancer, a type of cancer that is virtually incurable among humans and also dogs. In an article last year in the *Journal of the National Cancer Institute,* it was revealed that a study at Boston's Brigham and Women's Hospital of 89,000 women showed that women who ate high amounts of starch and didn't exercise regularly were 250% more likely than others to contract pancreatic cancer. Researchers examined starch intake as a factor in pancreatic cancer because previous research had shown that when an excessive amount of insulin is present in the pancreas, it enhances cancer cell growth in that organ. Starch foods, as you know, are notorious for increasing insulin levels.

The pancreas, of course, is also where the starch-digesting enzyme alpha amylase is produced. Therefore, it's also possible that excessive starch intake simply exhausts the pancreas and makes it more vulnerable to disease. At this point, these theories are merely speculative. However, twenty years ago, virtually *everything* about starch blockers was considered speculative.

Thus far, starch blockers have lived up to the potential they promised back in 1973, when Howard Hughes first saw an article about rats starving to death in Venezuela. Who can fully predict what promise they hold for the future?

Chapter Five

How To Tell
If Your Dog Is
Overweight

You'll Learn:

• Why overweight is not just a matter of weight – it's a matter of fat.

• Why there are no weight charts for dogs.

• Why some small dogs carry more fat than big dogs.

• **How to perform the same tests that Vets do!**

Pet owners are notorious for being blinded by love. They often see their animals only through the subjective perspective of affection, forgiving all flaws. This may be an emotionally healthy way to perceive an animal that you love – but it's not always best for the health of your animal.

To give your dog the best possible life, you need to be coldly objective about your dog's weight. If the dog is obese, you're not doing it a favor by thinking that it's pleasingly plump. In fact, this forgiving attitude can be very harmful to the dog. It can contribute to the dog being locked in a prison of fat that may someday kill it. Many dog guardians, though, are confused about knowing how to tell if their dogs are fat.

One reason they're confused is because there are no accurate, readily-available weight charts for various breeds of dogs. Dogs, perhaps even more than people, are very physically individualistic. For example, an amount of weight that is excessive on one collie might be perfectly acceptable on another, due to differences in size, bone structure, hormonal influences, ratios of fat to muscle, and lifestyle factors.

So let's go beyond the search for the proper "average" weight, and determine the proper weight for *your own particular dog*.
The best way to determine if your dog is overweight is to ignore scale weight, and to instead monitor body composition. Basically, you just *look* at your dog for fat deposits, and *feel* for fat deposits. If you find excessive fat, your dog needs to lose weight – regardless of how much it weighs compared to other dogs of the same breed.

Here is one of the best possible systems for determining proper weight in dogs. This system was derived from one developed by the Iams dog food company, which produces some of the best reduced-calorie dog foods.

IS YOUR DOG TOO HEAVY?

HERE'S WHAT TO LOOK FOR.

HEALTHY WEIGHT

- Feel your dog's back, along its vertebrae. The backbone is easy to feel; you can feel its bumps.

- Feel and look at your dog's pelvic area. The pelvic bones are easy to see, and when you touch them, they feel as if they are relatively close to the surface of the skin.

- Feel all around your dog's body. You shouldn't be able to find any notable deposits of fat. Your dog feels lean and muscular, and looks that way, too.

- Stand above your dog, and look at its waist, near its rear. The waist should be clearly visible, and significantly indented from the rest of the abdominal area.

- Next, look at your dog's abdomen from the side. The abdomen should be tucked up noticeably higher than the chest, or thoracic area. This is how you want your dog to look, and to feel, when you touch him or her.

Anything less than this signifies overweight. If your dog doesn't look and feel like this, it doesn't mean your dog is in danger – yet. But it does mean your dog is carrying too much fat, and being too fat – like other lifestyle risk factors – has, in effect, a life of its own: Fat builds on fat. Therefore, if your dog does not look and feel like this, intervene now, while it's still easy to dismantle the cycle of weight gain.

MODERATELY HEALTHY WEIGHT

- Look at your dog's ribs, and feel them. It will not be very easy to see each separate rib. They may be only lightly outlined against the surface of the skin.

- Next, feel for the ribs. Ribs are generally easier to feel than to see. If your dog is at a moderately healthy weight, you'll be able to feel each of its individual ribs.

- Feel all around your dog's body. In many places, you will feel a slight thickening under the skin indicating a small layer of fat. Even so, you probably won't be able to pinch that layer of fat, because there isn't enough of it to pinch.

- Look at your dog from above, checking its waist, near its rear. The waist is still there – you can see a moderate indentation.

- Look at your dog from the side, checking its abdomen, or belly. You can see that the abdomen is tucked up higher than the chest. However, the definition of the abdominal tuck is not striking. Your dog, in human terms, looks more like a weekend warrior than a true athlete.

This type of look is common among dogs, particularly as they age. It is not a sign of dangerous obesity. However, if your dog is still quite young, it shouldn't look and feel like this – it should look and feel leaner, and more defined. In all probability, your dog – even if its old – needs somewhat fewer calories and a little more exercise.

OVERWEIGHT

- You can feel your dog's ribs, but you can't see them. Your dog's sides look flat, with no protrusion of individual rib bones. When you feel the ribs, it's obvious to the touch that they are covered by a layer of fat.
- Looking at your dog from above, you can see that it still has a visible waist, but not much of one. His or her belly is beginning to pooch outwards, obscuring the waist.
- Look at your dog's abdomen from the side. The abdomen is tucked higher than the chest, but this abdominal tuck is not particularly obvious. The belly may be only an inch or two higher than the chest.
- Your dog, regardless of its actual age, doesn't have the lean and frisky look of a pup. It looks like a mature dog.

Many dogs can live in this condition for many years, without suffering notable decline or disease. However, this degree of over-weight is definitely problematic. It's a significant risk factor for many diseases. If your dog looks and feels like this, do something about it now. If you don't, you may end up fighting a serious disease at the same time you're trying to help your dog fight its weight. Don't let it go that far. Weight is a much harder battle at that stage.

OBESE

- You can't see your dog's ribs. They're buried beneath a layer of fat. However, you can still feel them. Even so, feeling individual ribs isn't easy – there's too much fat in the way.
- When you look at your dog from above, you can still see a slight indentation in the waist area. But this indentation is minor – maybe only an inch or so. Your dog's waist mostly looks rounded, like the waist of a significantly overweight person.
- Looking at your dog from the side, you can barely see that the abdomen is tucked higher than the chest. The belly is sagging. The belly looks overstuffed and sloppy.

Your dog is approaching the danger zone. This type of look and feel indicates enough obesity to invite any number of deadly disease: diabetes, cardiovascular disease, or cancer. Even if these awful diseases don't strike, your dog is almost certain to be suffering at least mild discomfort. He or she may have skin or coat problems, may be intolerant to heat, may have trouble breathing, may have limited stamina, and may be feeling the pain of joint disorders that are aggravated by excess weight.

If your dog could talk, it would ask you to help it lose weight. Your dog doesn't enjoy feeling like this. Furthermore, if your dog had any idea of how dangerous this extra weight was, it would go on a diet all by itself. Dogs are not innately self-destructive. They only destroy themselves with food when people let them.

DANGEROUSLY OBESE

- When you look for your dog's ribs, all you see is fat. The fat may be bunched into rings that encircle the dog, or it may sag downward. You can barely even feel the ribs. They're just too deeply buried in adipose tissue, or body fat.

- When you feel your dog throughout its body, you find lumps and layers of fat almost everywhere. The spine and tail area are covered with fat deposits. Muscle definition is completely obscured.

- You look down at your dog from above and wonder: "Where did his waist go?" If anything, the waist's indentation is now an outward bulge.

- Abdominal tuck? Forget about it! Your dog's belly actually hangs lower than its chest. The belly may even look distended, as if its been blown up with air.

You have a real problem on your hands. You need to get your dog on the starch blocker strategy as quickly as possible, and to gradually begin a serious exercise program. There is no way your dog will live in a healthy condition for its entire life expectancy if it is this fat.

Just be glad that starch blockers are now available. In the past, the only way you could have helped a dog that was dangerously obese would have been with food restriction. Your dog, in all probability, would've hated this – and would have let you know it every single day. Thank goodness there's now a better way.

In the next chapter, we'll tell you how to implement that better way. *It's easy!* That's why the next chapter is the shortest in the book.

Chapter Six

How To Use Canine Starch Blockers

You'll Learn:

- How much to give.
- When to give it.
- What to expect.

- **Why this approach is different from all others!**

It's time for your dog to start the starch blocker strategy.

Imagine you're coming in to a veterinary clinic to find out how to begin. Here are the questions you'll probably ask. These are the typical, nuts-and-bolts issues that people most often bring up as they prepare to help their dogs set out on this revolutionary approach to canine weight management.

Q. Can I give my dog starch blockers over a long period of time?

A. You can give them to your dog indefinitely, the same way you might give canine vitamins. People have taken starch blockers for years at a time with no ill effects, and there's no reason to expect that dogs would be harmed by long-term use. After your dog reaches its ideal weight, though, you may wish to reduce its use of starch blockers. Often, dogs who reach their ideal weights use starch blockers only once per day. This reduced use allows them to consume relatively more calories than they would be able to without taking starch blockers, thus making their mealtimes more pleasant and satisfying.

Q. How many starch blockers can my dog take?

A. The recommended dosage is one or two 500-mg. dosages with each meal, depending upon the size of your dog, and the size of its meals. That may be somewhat more than your dog needs, but because there are no significant side effects, and because starch blockers are inexpensive, some people give their dogs even larger dosages than this, just to be absolutely sure they're blocking as many starch calories as possible. Nonetheless, giving your large-breed dog more than three dosages at even a very high-starch meal is probably a waste of money. If your dog does take an excessive dosage, though, there will be no negative side effects, according to current safety studies.

Q. Should my dog take them with all meals, or just starchy meals?

A. They only work against starch, but most dog foods contain at least a small amount of starch, even if it's not obvious. The dog foods highest in starch are the dry, cereal-based foods. But even canned foods that look like meat often contain starch.

Q. If my dog gets more than the recommended dosage, will it lose more weight?

A. No, starch blockers only block the starch calories that are present at any one meal or snack and, for most starchy meals, one or two tablets will work as well as twenty-two.

Q. When do I give them to my dog?

A. Ideally, just before he or she eats. Fifteen to thirty minutes before is best. If you forget to give them prior to a meal, though, it's better to give them after your dog has already begun to eat than not to give them at all. When you do give them late, however, they're not as effective.

Q. Will it help my dog to skip meals?

A. No – it's counterproductive. We recommend that dogs eat regular meals. Eating regularly will stop your dog's body from going into the starvation mode of caloric hoarding. It will also keep your dog from being hungry.

Q. Isn't hunger a sign of weight loss?

A. No, it's just a sign of suffering. And if your dog suffers for too long, it will probably start eating more than it should. Being hungry doesn't make dogs thin. Being full does.

Q. Can exercise help my dog lose body fat?

A. Yes – especially on the starch blocker strategy. The strategy prevents excess storage of carbohydrates and therefore encourages your dog's body to burn body fat instead of stored carbs.

Q. Will my dog have to use starch blockers for the rest of its life?

A. It won't hurt him in any way if he does, because they don't have significant side-effects. However, his metabolism will probably respond to starch blockers by becoming more efficient, enabling him to use starch blockers much less frequently, particularly after he's reached his ideal weight. After his weight has been stabilized for an extended period of time, he might not need them at all.

Q. How will I know if my dog doesn't need them anymore?

A. If you become happy with your dog's weight, and happy with the diet it's eating, your dog won't need them. This is not an uncommon occurrence. It's more common, however, for people to see their dogs reach a weight they like, but still wish to continue to neutralize starch calories in order to be able to treat their dogs somewhat more indulgently, without causing them to gain weight.

Q. My dog has lost weight with a conventional low-calorie, high-fiber dog food. Can I combine starch blockers with that diet?

A. Yes. Starch blockers tend to work well with virtually all of the existing low-calorie, high-fiber dog foods. However, your dog can probably shift to a regular dog food, if you give it starch blockers, because the starch blockers will neutralize the starch calories in regular dog food.

Q. If my dog's weight hits a plateau, what should I do?

A. It's likely that your dog will hit plateaus occasionally and will stop losing weight for a week or more. If this persists for more than about three weeks, you should adjust your dog's ratio of calories metabolized versus calories burned. Your dog will have to eat less, exercise more, or neutralize more starch calories. Remember, the thinner your dog becomes, the fewer calories its body needs.

Q. If my dog uses starch blockers with metabolism-stimulating diet products, will it lose weight faster?

A. We don't recommend this at all. Stimulants, especially for dogs, are almost never effective for long-term weight management, and they have far too many negative side effects. Stick with a natural approach, and don't rush your dog's weight loss. If you rush it, your dog will regain weight much more easily. Don't experiment on an animal that you love.

Q. Are starch blockers available only through veterinarians?

A. No, they're an over-the-counter, non-prescription supplement. They're natural, nonstimulating, organic, nonallergenic for most dogs, and contain no herbs that have powerful drug-like effects.

Q. Where can I get them?

A. They're available at most pet food stores and at many veterinary clinics. Soon, they will probably be in almost every supermarket's pet section, just as they are now in almost every supermarket's health products section (for humans).

Q. Are some brands better than others?

A. At this point, we don't know about any cheap, knockoff ver-
   sions, such as ones that are just ground up beans. However,
   it's almost inevitable that these will eventually creep into the
   marketplace, possibly via less regulated venues, such as the
   Internet. To protect yourself from these brands – which
   have not been proven effective by clinical studies – buy only
   brands containing Phaseolamin 2250 (also called Phase 2™),
   which is the current most popular formula. This designation
   will be listed on the label. This is the standardized formula
   that has been widely clinically tested. To the best of our
   knowledge, no other formulas, at the time of publication of
   this book, have been clinically tested, with results reported
   in a scientific journal.

Q. I don't like to solve problems with pills. Don't starch blockers
   make losing weight too easy? Whatever happened to discipline
   and willpower?

A. Starch blockers make weight loss easier, but it will still be a
   challenge for your dog. You've still got to control your dog's
   fat and sugar intake, and your dog will still have to exercise.
   Starch blockers work with a healthy lifestyle – they don't
   take the place of it.

Q. My dog's veterinarian is curious about starch blockers. How
   can she learn more about the scientific details?

A. She can read synopses of some of the safety and weight loss
   studies at www.starchstopper.com.

Q. Can starch blockers be taken with prescription drugs,
   without causing problems?

A. They have no known interactions with any prescription
   drugs.

Q. My dog has diabetes. Can I count on starch blockers to keep her blood sugar stable?

A. Because diabetes can have deadly consequences, complete reliance upon starch blockers would be very unwise. For example, what if your dog ate more starch than you thought she had, or maybe got her starch blocker a little bit too late in the meal? For most healthy dogs, these mistakes would be inconsequential. For dogs with diabetes, they could be very problematic. Therefore, if your dog has diabetes, you should wait for more testing to be done, and for a protocol to be established. In the meantime, your dog still might benefit from starch blockers and might be able to enjoy a more varied diet containing more starch (if you neutralize the starch calories). But do not stop testing your dog's blood sugar levels and do not alter your dog's medical use of insulin without specific, explicit orders from your veterinarian.

Q. What's the easiest type of starch blocker to give to a dog?

A. Anything but a pill. It's usually hard to get dogs to take pills. Most brands of canine starch blockers are in powder or chew form. If all you have are capsules, open them and sprinkle them on your dog's food. If all you have are tablets, crush them and mix them into food. Remember, though, to give them about 15 minutes prior to the main portion of the meal.

Q. What about my cat? Can he take starch blockers?

A. It might be unwise, because no well-documented research has been done specifically on cats. However, we do know that cats require starch even less than dogs do – they can subsist entirely on meat. We also know that starch blockers have never shown any toxic effects. Furthermore, a great meany cats are dangerously overweight. Even so, we prefer to be cautious.

Chapter Seven

Diet For A Perfect Dog Like Yours!

You'll Learn:

- Why most bargain dog foods aren't a bargain.
- What's in most dog foods.
- Why some dog foods contain the most expensive water you'll ever buy.

- **How starch blockers can bring pleasure back to your dog's mealtime!**

Feed Your Dog Right

Feeding your dog can be easy, if you're using the starch blocker strategy. The strategy enables you to feed your dog normal foods in normal portions, thus helping to keep your dog satisfied and happy.

Without starch blockers, it's far harder. The main reason it's harder is simply because dogs, like people, love to eat. For a person – or a dog – consuming food means more than just fulfilling physical requirements: It's not the same as just putting more gas in your car's tank. Dogs, as well as people, eat for pleasure, and often keep eating even after they have fulfilled their body's physical requirements. Also, dogs often perceive food from their guardians as symbols of the guardian's love, and this makes the food even more attractive. In addition, dogs sometimes eat out of boredom, and eat out of habit.

All of these forces frequently make dogs eat somewhat more than they should. If this happens only rarely, it doesn't create weight problems. However, these forces are at work every day of the week. Therefore, overeating tends to happen frequently, and pounds gradually pile on.

As dogs gain weight, they generally eat even more. Overeating is a self-reinforcing habit. When they do eat more, their extra food is usually in the form of high-carb, cereal-based dog foods. This creates further problems. It exacerbates the destabilization of their metabolisms, and it makes dogs crave even *more* carbs. Soon, a constant cycle of overeating is established – and this cycle can be hard to break.

More than any other approach, though, use of starch blockers has been proven to stop this cycle.

- It lowers the carb calories in foods, and helps dogs lose weight.

- It helps a dog's metabolism to repair itself, and to recover from the damage of carbohydrate destabilization.

- It allows dogs to eat normal volumes of regular food, which keeps them from feeling hungry.

- It allows guardians to safely give their dogs generous amounts of calorie-neutralized foods and snacks, which dogs often perceive as symbols of their guardian's love.

Therefore, the starch blocker strategy makes it far easier to feed dogs a prudent, sensible diet.

For most dogs, this diet is based largely around commercial dog foods. As a rule, these foods are high in cereals. Without starch blockers, these high-grain dog foods can sometimes create problems. *With starch blockers, though, even high-grain dog foods can be healthy.*

What About Snacks?

A good rule of thumb is that snacks shouldn't comprise more than 10% of your dog's daily diet. More than that will interfere with your dog's feeding schedule. Also, if you're ever going to splurge on high-quality, nutritious, expensive products for your dog, spend it on wholesome snacks. The cheapest dog biscuits and treats are just too high in carbs. If you do give high-carb snacks -- <u>don't forget the starch blockers!</u>

Feeding Dogs With Conventional Dog foods

Standard, cereal-based dog foods have a lot of good things in them: protein, essential fatty acids, abundant vitamins and minerals, and excellent amounts of fiber. There's only one thing wrong with most of them: They're often too high in starch. *Starch blockers solve that.* They neutralize about two-thirds to three-fourths of all the starch calories, but don't reduce the protein, vitamins, minerals, essential fatty acids, or fibers. *In effect, they eliminate the bad and leave the good.*

This is great for your dog's health. It's also good for your own budget. Here's why: Cereal-based dog foods took over the American pet foods industry primarily because they're so much cheaper than meat-based foods. Even the cheapest meat costs more than corn and wheat. These days, in the "Atkins Era," some dog guardians probably feel as if they owe it to their dogs to feed them a meat-based diet, instead of a grain-based diet. But who can afford it? Atkins-style eating can be expensive for people, and it's almost as costly for pets.

Fortunately, starch blockers solve this problem. They transform a cereal-based, high-protein, high-fiber, high-carb diet into a high-protein, high-fiber, *low-carb diet*.

Even when you add in the cost of starch blockers, using them is still by far the most economical way of providing a high-protein, low-carb diet for your dog. This diet should probably be centered on one of the premium brands of dry dog foods, or kibble. Why premium? Because it's healthier – and because it can be just as cost-effective, in the long run.

Bargain dog foods sometimes end up costing more – because you have to use more.

Bargain dog foods are often cheaper because their ingredients just aren't as packed with good nutrients as premium brands.

- They often have too many fillers – foodstuffs that are not digestible.
- They often use lower-quality ingredients, such as soy protein and bone meal, instead of meat.
- They frequently include ingredients that don't taste very good, so the manufacturers try to cover up this taste with excessive artificial flavors and colorings.
- Their lower nutritional values often mean they don't satisfy a dog's hunger.

In fact, you might end up using almost twice as much of a low-quality dog food, just to keep your dog from whining with hunger.

To find a high-quality dog food at a reasonable price, you will need to learn to read dog food labels, just as you now probably read the labels on the foods you put into your own body. Here are some guidelines.

The Best Foods Don't Use Adjective "Qualifiers" In The Product Name.

If the label just says "Beef Dog Food," instead of something like "Beef Dinner Dog food," or "Beef Formula Dog food," it contains 95% beef.

Next Best Are Brands That Do Use Qualifiers In The Descriptions.

If the label says "Dinner," "Formula," or "Nuggets," it means that the main ingredient comprises 25% of the food. Sometimes, though, labels get a little tricky, and say "Beef and Rice Formula." This means it may not be 25% beef. It's 25% beef *plus* rice, and the beef can be as little as 3% of the total.

Try To Avoid Food Labels That Contain The Word "With."

If the label says something like "Healthy Doggy Dinner With Beef," the beef only has to make up 3% of the total.

Watch Out For The Word "Flavored."

That word promises virtually nothing. Your dog's "Lamb Flavored Formula" might have only a microscopic amount of lamb in it.

What About Canned Food?

These same labeling laws also apply to canned dog foods. Therefore, it may surprise you to discover that your dog's canned food - which certainly *looks* like meat - might be mostly cereal. Check the label - and if it does contain a substantial number of carbs, give your dog starch blockers with it, no matter how much it may look like meat.

You can be certain, though, that regardless of how much meat there is in canned food, *the main ingredient is water*. Water comprises an average of about 74% to 78% of the entire weight of most cans of dog food. Also, canned foods tend to be relatively high in calories, in part because of fat that is added to them. They average about 500 calories in each 14-15 ounce can.

Canned foods also frequently have a relatively high amount of salt.

To your dog, this all sounds pretty tasty: fat, salt, water, cereal and meat! Shaped and flavored! Bring it on! Canned foods are known for their palatability. But don't let your dog's affection for this food convince you that it's the best possible thing your pet can be eating. Lots of things that taste good, to dogs as well as people, aren't very healthy.

Therefore, you should shop carefully when choosing canned foods, just as you do when buying dry foods. As a rule, the higher quality canned foods will cost more, but may ultimately be more cost effective, because they'll enable you to feed your dog less volume. They may also help you to avoid veterinary costs associated with complications of obesity.

What About Table Scraps?
All depends. Scraps of what? Lean meat? Or creampuffs?
If the food from your table is healthy, high-protein fare, it might
be the healthiest thing your dog will eat that day.
But remember -- calories do count, so don't overdo it.

Calories Count

Calories are an extremely important element of weight management. They're not the only relevant factor, of course. Carb calories, for example, will tend to disrupt your dog's metabolism more than protein calories, and will therefore probably trigger more weight gain. Even so, calories are crucially relevant. The primary benefit of starch blockers is simply that they *reduce the body's intake of calories*. This is even more important than the role they plan in reducing insulin spikes.

It can be hard, though, to figure out the number of calories in conventional dog foods, because their labels can be even harder to read than the labels on human foods. It can require a little detective work. Frequently, dog food labels only express their content in weight, by grams, and you have to ascertain the number of calories yourself. For example, a label might say that one serving of a food is:

- 26 grams of protein
- 45 grams of carbohydrates
- 15 grams of fat

To figure out the calories, you need to know that there are 4 calories in every gram of protein and carbohydrate, and 9 calories in every gram of fat. Therefore, the total calories would be:

- 4 x 26 grams of protein   =   104 calories
- 4 x 45 grams of carbohydrates   =   180 calories
- 9 x 15 grams of fat   =   135 calories

               Total Calories   =   419 calories

This would be a relatively high number of calories for a small dog to eat at one meal, or for a large dog who had a larger portion of it. However, when you eliminate all the starch calories that are neutralized by starch blockers, it reduces the total number of calories dramatically. If 75% of the carbohydrate calories, all from starch, were to be neutralized, the calorie count would be reduced by 135 calories, from 419 to 284.

What a difference!

This is more than enough caloric reduction to transform this feeding into a prudent, low-carb, high-protein, low-calorie meal for most dogs.

As you can clearly see, starch blockers provide a huge advantage, by changing a high-carb meal of conventional dog food into a healthier low-carb meal. But starch blockers alone are not the entire answer to canine weight management. Exercise is also critically important.

So that's how we'll end this book – by showing you how important it is to get your dog moving, in order to burn off all the calories it eats!

Chapter Eight

See Spot Run!

You'll Learn:

- Why dogs are programmed by evolution to require exercise.
- Why even carefully fed dogs can become overweight if they don't exercise.
- Why a dog's body burn stored carbohydrates before it burns body fat.

- **How starch blockers supercharge exercise!**

Exercise and Evolution

Dogs, as you probably know, are directly descended from wolves. They evolved as a species to live in the wild, and for eons they needed to hunt down or forage for every single bite they ate. When winter came, they walked to a warmer sanctuary. When larger animals threatened them, they ran for their lives. They roamed the mountains and prairies. They stayed *active*!

Their level of activity remained high even after they were domesticated by humans. Until just the past fifty or so years, most dogs were depended upon by their owners to fulfill important tasks. A great many of them lived in rural areas, just as most people, until relatively recently, lived in rural areas. These dogs helped herd sheep. They helped hunt game animals. They kept rodents and other pests from destroying crops and infesting barns. Often, they had to find their own food, in the wild, to supplement the meager table scraps they were offered. They ate almost no grain, in part because dogs, unlike people, require no carbohydrates to survive.

This basic lifestyle – requiring high levels of activity – endured during evolution for hundreds of thousands of years.

And then it came to a screeching halt, about twenty to fifty years ago – at the same basic time that the weights of dogs began to rise.

In the more recent years of the last century, as people increasingly left rural life, dogs moved indoors. They were no longer valuable contributors to the family welfare. They were... pets. Pampered, pudgy pets. On the surface, this probably seemed like a good deal to many dog guardians. After all, isn't it better for dogs to lie on a warm carpet all day long, nibbling kibble, than to have to kill rodents and run down rabbits just to survive? Actually, no. It's not better.

Dogs were created by the forces of nature to be active, and almost anything that directly contradicts nature bodes ill for those who engage in it.

Dogs themselves *prefer* the rough and tumble life of the outdoors to the sedentary security of indoor life. Sure, dogs can learn to be lazy, just like people can, but with only a little urging, almost any dog will leap at the chance to go for a walk – and better yet, a run.

This affinity for exercise is the genetic heritage of the animals we love, and we have a responsibility as their guardians to provide them with at least some access to this heritage.

Not just because they enjoy it. But because they *need* it, in order to stay free from the diseases that sedentary lifestyles contribute to. It's hard to keep your dog at a healthy weight without exercise. Here's why:

The Many Effects of Exercise On Your Dog

1. <u>Exercise oxidizes calories.</u> It burns them faster than any other physiological action. An easy-to-remember equation on exercise and fat loss for humans is: One hour of exercise each day burns one pound of fat each week. This rate is somewhat similar among dogs.

2. <u>Exercise reduces your dog's insulin levels</u>. It increases insulin sensitivity (the ability of cells to respond to insulin). This decreases the need for excessive insulin output. In addition, exercise burns body fat, and the less fat your dog has, the less insulin it will produce. When there's less insulin in your dog's system, it's body is more prone to *burn* fat, instead of *store* it. Even when dogs don't lose weight, exercise still reduces their vulnerability to diabetes.

3. <u>Exercise increases your dog's muscle mass, which boosts calorie burning.</u> Muscle tissue burns fat approximately 10% to 20% more efficiently than any other body tissue, including body fat. This occurs even when the muscles aren't in active use!

4. <u>Exercise decreases your dog's appetite</u>. Conventional wisdom says that a good workout increases hunger, but science says it doesn't. The hormones and neurotransmitters associated with exercise all have a stimulating effect on your dog's body and help control hunger. To contribute to hunger, exercise must be prolonged

for several hours, thoroughly depleting glycogen, as well as most accessible body-fat storage areas.

5. <u>Exercise improves general health.</u>   Everybody knows exercise helps prevent cardiovascular disease, one of the primary fatal diseases among dogs. What many people don't know is that it also helps prevent minor illnesses, by boosting immunity. Also, among humans, it's been proven that exercise reduces the risk of cancer of the reproductive organs by 250%, the risk of breast cancer by 200%, and the risk of colon cancer by 67%. It also significantly reduces chronic pain.   Obviously, not all of these benefits are directly related to canine weight management. But they're certainly all related to health, and when optimal health is achieved, fat loss will tend to occur naturally, as an almost unavoidable consequence.

The Best News Yet

This book has been full of good news: proven facts about starch blockers that will improve the life of your dog, and improve your life as its guardian. Here's some of the best news yet: Starch blockers have a profoundly positive impact upon exercise. Starch blockers will amplify your dog's exercise. They'll turbo charge it. They will make your dog's exercise easier – by knocking off extra pounds – and even more importantly, they will make exercise more *effective*.

Starch blockers make exercise more effective by encouraging your dog's body to *rely upon body fat* as a primary source of fuel. When your dog's body becomes accustomed to looking for energy from body fat, instead of carbohydrates, it becomes more efficient in its use of exercise. For example, a dog who's not taking starch blockers might burn about two ounces of body fat from an hour of brisk walking, but a dog taking starch blockers might burn three or more ounces. Over the course of a month, when all physical activity is taken into account, this degree of difference can have a huge impact upon fat loss.

This accelerated fat loss among dogs on starch blockers occurs for two essential reasons.

First: Dogs who do not take starch blockers almost always have more stored carbohydrates in their systems than dogs who do. These stored carbs, called glycogen, are found in the dog's liver and the muscles. Your dog's body loves to use glycogen for energy, because it's so easy to burn. It's basically just predigested, pure calories, waiting to be used.

Athletes in endurance events often try to increase their levels of glycogen in order to have an easy source of fuel to burn throughout their events. They do this by eating high amounts of carbohydrates, a practice that's called carbo-loading.

This is a smart tactic for running a marathon, but it's the exact opposite of what a dog trying to lose weight wishes to achieve. Dogs who are trying to lose fat want to burn as little glycogen as possible, and proceed straight to body-fat burning as quickly as possible. The only realistic way to do this is for a dog to have a limited amount of glycogen in its system. Starch blockers are uniquely adept at helping dogs lower their glycogen levels, by blocking unnecessary dietary carbohydrates.

Carb-loading doesn't even work for dogs. Some sled dog competitors recently tried to carbo-load their dogs before races, but it backfired. Instead of providing more energy, it caused the dogs' muscles to tighten painfully from excess lactic acid, a condition known as rhabdomyolysis.

Thus, to get the maximum efficiency out of your dog's body, and to attain the optimal result from exercise, focus on carb-*unloading*, instead of carb-loading.

The second major reason why dogs taking starch blockers achieve accelerated fat loss from exercise is that their bodies become *biochemically trained to rely upon body fat as a primary source of energy*. When dogs are not taking starch blockers and are eating typically high amounts of starch, their bodies become accustomed to burning carbohydrates first, and body fat significantly later. This hierarchy of fuel preference changes, though, when significant amounts of starch calories are neutralized. The body of a dog taking starch blockers is relatively less dependent upon glycogen for fuel, and also is less dependent upon dietary carbs, dietary proteins, and dietary fats. After two or more weeks of consistent starch blocker use, the body of a dog taking starch blockers becomes singularly capable of focusing upon body fat as fuel. Within individual cells, fat-burning is heightened, as the cells' fuel-transforming mitochondria achieve maximum efficiency.

For many centuries, this degree of responsiveness to exercise was very much the norm among dogs. When our dogs' canine ancestors were physically active, as they were so much of the time, they saw the results of exercise almost immediately, much the same way, for example, that a puppy with a still-undamaged carb metabolism might respond quickly to exercise.

However, as America's reliance upon high-carb dog foods has become entrenched as the dietary standard over the past fifty years, the efficiency of exercise among many dogs has declined. It's now common for dogs on high-carb diets to exercise strenuously on a regular basis, but still be overweight. Much of the time, even when they exercise, they burn only glycogen and dietary calories (especially carbs), rather than body fat.

Your dog's natural responsiveness to exercise can usually be restored in as little as two to three weeks, with robust starch calorie neutralization.

What Exercise Is Best?

Whatever *you* want to do is best. Dogs will go along with just about anything. They'll just be happy to be outdoors, using the strong, sinewy bodies that nature gave them. Unless your dogs are old, ill, or injured, it will be difficult for you to wear them out before they wear you out. For example, border collies preparing for sheep herding competitions often cover up to 100 miles per day in training. Sled dogs typically trot at about 10 miles per hour for 10 to 14 hours each day during a race. Greyhounds hit a top speed of about 50 miles per hour during a sprint. So don't worry about your dog. Worry about yourself.

The primary concern you should have for your dog is just making sure he or she doesn't overdo it in the early stages of an exercise program. Start slowly, and build up intensity gradually, just as you would in your own exercise program. Also be careful when you're exercising your dog during hot weather. Dogs playing in the heat can become dehydrated and suffer heat stroke when they're excited about their play; they don't always have the instinct to avoid it. If your dog is running hard in hot weather, make him or her rest occasionally, and be vigilant about providing enough water.

Other than that, go for it! Run with your dog. Ride your bike while your dog runs. Play Frisbee with her. Play fetch. Go hunting. Go swimming. Teach her tricks. Take her sledding. Have her pull you on skis, if she's big enough. Go backpacking with your dog. Build her a backyard obstacle course.

Above all: *walk your dog.* This is good for your dog. It's good for you. And it's good for the bond you share. Try to walk your dog an hour every day. That may seem like a lot, but it's far less physical work than your dog's evolutionary ancestors did – and far less than your *own* ancestors did. If you can make this level of commitment to your dog's health – *and to your own health* – it will be one of the wisest decisions you ever made.

It will make you and your dog healthy.

It will make you and your dog happy.

It will make you and your dog closer.

And in the final analysis, isn't closeness the best thing about having a dog?

THE LAST WORD

We truly believe that buying this little book was one of the best investments you ever made in supporting the health of the dog that you love.

This may sound grandiose – but think about it.

Before you read this book, were you aware of how dangerous it can be for your dog to be overweight? And even if you were aware, did you know what to do about it?

Most people don't know. Even most of the best veterinarians in America have been unable to solve the terrible problem of canine obesity.

That's because most people and most veterinarians have not known, until quite recently, about the proven value of the starch blocker strategy for dogs.

Starch blockers, when combined with a prudent diet and adequate exercise, provide the most extraordinary approach ever devised to solve the problem of canine obesity.

They represent the future of weight management in companion animals.

Welcome to that future.

Addendum One

The Studies

Following are two studies on canine weight
management with starch blockers.

Due to copyright restraints, the Mayo Clinic study
is presented in its brief format.

A Study

Use of Commercial Starch Blockers in Canine Weight Loss
Steven Rosenblatt, MD, Ph.D; Curtis Willauer, VMD
Annette Timmel, DVM; Barbara Ota, MS

INTRODUCTION

A recent study published in 2003 showed that 25% of dogs in the United States were overweight and many were classified as obese (1). This is a startling increase since a similar study in 1985 (2). The reasons for this large increase in companion animal obesity is not readily apparent but it is similar to the rise in human overweight and obesity rates (3).

One postulated reason for this weight gain is the increased uses of starch carbohydrate additives to commercial dog and pet foods. Additionally, many dogs are fed table scraps by their families which often consist of starch products. Since the canine digestive tract is designed to digest and assimilate mostly protein, the addition of a significant percentage of starch carbohydrates into the diet will be stored as fat, often in the abdominal area. This increase in weight is one of the major causes of the sudden rise of diabetes, heart disease, musculoskeletal problems and cancers in the canine population.

This is a common problem often found in human weight loss clinics. The most effective solution to human weight loss seems to be the "low carb" diets. This is most typified in the "Atkins Diet." A newer and more effective addition to this diet program is the introduction of starch blockers which effectively block the digestion of starch and thus the absorption of starch calories into the body.

Starch blockers were originally developed in the 1970s and 1980s as a natural way to block the digestive enzyme alpha-amylase which converts starch to simple sugars. Without the action of alpha-amylase, starch is not broken down into sugar and thus cannot be absorbed into the body (4).

The action of starch blockers was first developed using an animal model (5,6) and several studies have been done on the mechanism of action and effectiveness in canines (7,8). It was for this reason that the current study decided to investigate the clinical application of the use of starch blockers in canine populations that were seen at outpatient veterinary clinics.

PROCEDURE

Two outpatient veterinary clinics were used in this multicenter design. Both clinics were located in Hawaii, one on the island of Maui, the other on the Big Island of Hawaii. Dogs were enrolled in the study who were deemed by the attending veterinarian to be overweight or obese. Each dog was examined by the veterinarian on an initial visit. At this time an initial evaluation form was completed which consisted of a physical exam and laboratory exams including a blood test and fecal float test. Each dog was weighed in and the abdominal girth measured at the navel was recorded. In addition a subjective evaluation scale was completed by the clinic doctor or staff.

At the time of the initial visit client instruction sheets were given to the dog owners which explained the purpose of the study and the procedure to be followed. Each owner was given enough starch blocker capsules for one week and asked to return with their animal in one week. Owners were instructed not to change their dog's exercise or food program.

Animals were seen for eight consecutive weekly visits following the initial visit. At each visit the dog was weighed and measured by the clinic staff. A subjective clinical evaluation was also filled out at each visit. After the eight visits, second blood and fecal samples were taken on the dogs and sent for analysis.

Product and Dosage

The starch blocker product utilized in this study is a white kidney bean extract developed and produced by VetMedicinals, Inc. The trade name of the product is "VetSlim." Quality control testing at the factory assured high purity and consistency of the product.

The product was supplied in capsules each containing 500 mg of the Phase 2™. Owners were instructed to open the capsules and sprinkle them on the food (but not to mix it into the food) before the dog began to eat.

Owners were instructed to sprinkle the contents of one 500 mg capsule on the food if the dog's body weight is less than 50 pounds. Owners were to sprinkle two 500 mg capsules on the food if the dog weighed 50 pounds or more.

<u>Canine Subjects</u>

Ten dogs were required from each of the two clinics. They were of different breeds and all judged to be overweight or obese by the attending veterinarian. The breed of each dog is listed in the results section of the study. Twenty dogs were initially enrolled in the study.

RESULTS AND ANALYSIS

Of the twenty dogs that were enrolled in the study one dropped out after the initial visit due to travel concerns. Two other dogs dropped out after three visits due to time requirements needed to be seen for clinical evaluation. Seventeen dogs completed the entire nine weeks of the study. The weekly measures for all 19 dogs is contained in the appendix, including the partial results for the two dogs who dropped out in the middle of the study.

Out of the 17 animals that completed the study 15 lost weight as a result of the starch blocker product (VetSlim). Without any change in diet or exercise, 88% of the subject dogs lost weight. This is significant on a two-tailed p test of p> .01.

The average weight loss in all dogs in the study is 1.91 pounds and represents a 3.07% average body weight loss per dog.

If we analyze the 15 dogs who lost weight the average weight loss per dog is 3.01 pounds. This represents an average weight loss of 4.61% per dog.

In looking at the abdominal girth measurements none of the dogs gained inches. Even those few dogs who gained weight either lost inches at the waist or stayed the same. Of the 15 dogs who lost weight in the study, 13 of them also lost inches. Two dogs who lost weight stayed the same in abdominal measurement. **The average abdominal girth lost was 1.44 inches per dog.**

Examination of the blood test, done pre and post-treatment, revealed no change in relevant measures. There was no change in liver enzyme measures or in digestive enzyme levels. The fecal float measure showed no change in fecal fat composition and no intestinal parasites before and after the study.

DISCUSSION

The use of starch blockers in animal weight loss has been demonstrated in several previous studies. These studies done at the Gastrointestinal Research Unit of the Mayo Clinic, demonstrated that starch blockers were effective at causing amylase inhibition and thus preventing the digestion of starch products (7,8). This current study is the first to look at the use of starch blockers in a clinical setting.

Several points need to be discussed in an initial study such as this one. First of all it should be emphasized that a study of this type only shows changes in weight as a result of the starch blocker. Even though the dogs on average lost almost 5% of their body weight with the starch blocker alone, it does not incorporate dietary changes or an increased exercise program. Both of these changes along with the starch blockers is a much more effective way to achieve weight loss. By holding other variables constant and only including the starch blocker we have focused only on the effect of blocking the starch component of the diet but not on any other aspects of a well-rounded weight loss program as might be found in a clinical setting. Dietary change, exercise, AND starch blockers are all important parts of a comprehensive weight loss program.

Secondly, from a procedural point of view this study probably understated the weight loss potential of the starch blockers. Owners were instructed to empty the contents of the capsules directly on the food. Studies in human weight loss showed better results if the product was taken about 15 minutes before the meal in order to allow the starch blocker to precede the food into the small intestine and thus inactivate the alpha-amylase preventing the digestion and absorption of starch. In future studies we will be investigating a chewable dog-biscuit type product that will be given before each meal in order to give the active starch blocker ingredient time to reach the stomach and small intestine before the food is consumed.

Thirdly, it was noticed by some of the investigators that the larger dogs may need a larger quantity of starch blocker. It was suggested that because of the faster transit time of food in the gut in canine animals the need for larger amounts of the starch blocker are needed to inactivate a sufficient amount of alpha-amylase. In future studies we propose that dogs over 80 pounds be given 1.5 grams of starch blocker before each meal.

Finally it should be pointed out that out of the 19 dogs in the study, even the dogs that did not complete the study, 15 of them lost abdominal girth as measured around the navel. None of the animals showed an increase in waist size, even those who gained a small amount of weight. All animals lost waist size or stayed the same. This finding is similar to human studies where participants lost not only weight but also inches at the waist (9). This indicates that in place of using starch for energy production the body is burning body fat. This is seen to be one of the major factors in the use of starch blockers for weight loss. By blocking starch carbohydrates the body is forced to burn its stored energy in the form of body fat. This study in canine weight loss seems to confirm this finding.

The successful use of starch blocker in this group of dogs seems to warrant even larger investigations of this approach in helping to combat the growing problem of increasing obesity in our canine population.

REFERENCES

1. Report from the National Academy of Sciences, September 2003.

2. Report from the National Academy of Science, "Nutrient Requirements for Dogs," 1985.

3. Mokdad, A. H., et al., "The Spread of the Obesity Epidemic in the United States, 1991-1998, "*Journal of the American Medical Association*, No. 282, 1999.

4. Rosenblatt, S., and Stauth, C., *The Starch Blocker Diet*, Pub: HarperCollins, 2003.

5. Yamadera, K., et al., Mayo Clinic, "Can Chronic Ingestion of a Wheat Amylase Inhibitor Reduce Insulin Secretion Without Producing Malabsorption in Dogs?" *Pancreas*, Vol. 7, No. 6, p. 762, 1992.

6. Umoren, J. and Kies, C., Northern Illinois University, "Commercial Soybean Starch Blocker Coinsumption: Impact on Weight Gain and on Copper, Lead, and Zinc Status of Rats," *Plant Foods in Human Nutrition*, Vol. 42, No. 2, 1992.

7. Koike, D., et al., "Effect of a Wheat Amylase Inhibitor on Canine Carbohydrate Digestion, Gastrointestinal Function, and Pancreatic Growth," *Gastroenterology*, Vol. 108, No. 4, 1995.

8. Tonho, H., et al., "Intrailcal Carbohydrate Regulates Canine Postprandial Pancreaticobiliary Secretion and Upper Gut Motility," Gastroenterology, Vol. 109, No. 6. 1995.

9. Udani, J., "Investigation of the Efficacy of Phase 2™ Starch Blockers," Publication pending, 2002.

A STUDY

Gastroenterology
December 1995 * Volume 109 * Number 6

Intraileal carbohydrate regulates canine postprandial pancreaticobiliary secretion and upper gut motility.
E. P. DiMagno, M.D., The Mayo Clinic
Published in: Gastroenterology

BACKGROUND & AIMS

The effect of nutrients in the distal small intestine or colon on postprandial upper gut function is incompletely understood. The aim of this study was to determine if carbohydrate in the ileum or proximal colon of dogs affects postprandial pancreaticobiliary secretion, gastrointestinal, and circulating concentrations of certain gastrointestinal regulatory peptides.

METHODS

Seven dogs were prepared with permanent infusion and aspiration catheters in the duodenum and ileum and an infusion catheter in the caecum. Coincident with eating a meal containing liquid and solid markers, ileal or colonic (n = 5 dogs for each) fusion were begun of isosmolar 0.9% NaCt or carbohydrate in a 3.1 ratio of starch to glucose. Pancreatic enzyme output, bile acid delivery, gastrointestinal polypeptide, and plasma concentrations of pancreatic polypeptide, neurotensin, and peptide YY were measured for 6 hours postprandially.

RESULTS

Carbohydrate infusion in the ileum, but not in the proximal colon, increased amylase secretion and plasma peptide YY, slowed gastric emptying of liquids and solids, slowed small intestinal transit, and decreased bile acid delivery into the duodenum (p < 0.05 in each).

CONCLUSIONS

Carbohydrate in the ileum regulates postprandial exocrine pancreatic enzyme secretion and other postprandial upper gut functions. Peptide YY may play a role int his regulation.

(Gastroenterology 1995 Dec; 109(6): 1977-85)

Notes:

Notes:

_____

_____

_____

_____

_____

_____

_____

_____

_____

_____

_____

_____

_____

_____

_____

_____

_____

_____

Notes:

Notes:

_____

_____

_____

_____

_____

_____

_____

_____

_____

_____

_____

_____

_____

_____

_____

_____

_____

_____

Notes:

Quick Order Form

<u>Fax orders:</u> 310-551-2724 Send this form.

<u>Telephone orders:</u> Call 800-923-9074 toll free.

    Have your credit card ready.

<u>Email orders:</u> info@sierramed.com

<u>Postal Orders:</u> SierraMed Publishing, 2029 Century Park East, Suite 1112, Los Angeles, CA 90067 Telephone: 310-226-2555

Please send the following books.

_____

_____

_____

_____

Please send more FREE information on:

☐ Other Books ☐ Speaking/Seminars ☐ Pet Products
☐ News Letter

Name:_____

Address:_____

City:_____State:____ Zip:_____

Telephone: (_____) _____

Email address:_____

Sales tax: Please add 8.25% for products shipped to California addresses.

Shipping: <u>By air U.S.</u> $4.00 for first book and $2.00 for each additional product. <u>International</u>: $9.00 for first book $5.00 for each additional product (estimate).

Payment:

☐ Check ☐ Credit Card ☐ Visa ☐ MasterCard ☐ AMEX

Card number:_____

Name on card:_____

Exp. Date:_____